*Your Developmentally
Retarded Child Can Communicate*

Books by Julia S. Molloy

Teaching the Retarded Child to Talk
Trainable Children: *Curriculum and Procedures*

Your Developmentally Retarded Child Can Communicate

A Guide for Parents and Teachers
in Speech, Language,
and Nonverbal Communication

Julia S. Molloy
Former Principal, Orchard School and
Julia S. Molloy Education Center,
Professor of Special Education,
University of San Diego

and Arlene Matkin
Principal, Julia S. Molloy Education Center

With a Foreword by Paul Moore
University of Florida, Gainesville

The John Day Company   New York

Library of Congress Cataloging in Publication Data

Molloy, Julia Sale.
    Your developmentally retarded child can communicate.

    (John Day books in special education)
    Bibliography: p.
    Includes index.
    1. Mentally handicapped children—Education—Language arts. 2. Mentally handicapped children—Language. I. Matkin, Arlene M., joint author. II. Title.
LC4616.M64   1975   371.9′28   75-9982
ISBN 0-381-97102-3

10 9 8 7 6 5 4 3 2 1

Acknowledgments

OUR SINCERE THANKS to the parents and teachers of our special children. Through their cooperation, interest, encouragement, and confidence so much has been made possible.

And to the children, who make it all worthwhile, we owe abiding gratitude.

A very special award is due our ever-patient typist, Katharine Clark Reilly.

JULIA S. MOLLOY
ARLENE MATKIN

Contents

Foreword

MOST PARENTS ARE RELATIVELY UNAWARE of retarded development until they are confronted by the problem in one of their own children. Then they learn that there are many with this impairment, that retarded development occurs in families of both rich and poor, educated and uneducated, and among all races. They also learn that much can be done to help the affected persons. However, no one who is realistic will attempt to ignore or minimize the distress that exists in the thousands of families who have a child with retarded development. Nor can one fail to sympathize with the extraordinary living and learning problems which face the retarded child and his family. Yet the crucial problems associated with serious delay in the development of communication skills can be greatly reduced by the deft, practical, and friendly guidance provided by experts such as the authors of this book. No longer do parents need to feel lost or unable to help their children. The writers have been through it all hundreds of times; they have studied the impairment in all of its aspects; and they have worked with the children and their parents. They know what can and should be done from firsthand experience. Furthermore, the newer theoretical and pedagogical developments in speech and language learning, which they apply in their university teaching, are fundamental also in their book.

The reader will recognize that this volume is organized to progress from basic principles and concepts in the development of language and speaking, to specific, practical steps which parents and communication therapists can follow independently or in concert. Suggestions are specific and concrete. Chapters are short. They focus upon the development of communication skills which provide the route to most other accomplishments. The authors emphasize the fact that the child who understands words spoken to him learns more rapidly, is easier to teach, responds more readily, and assumes a more normal place within his family. They also stress that patient, persistent, persevering instruction will usually provide rewarding progress.

The professional worker in the field of speech and language rehabilitation will sense the authoritative, unequivocal approach of the presentation. He will also recognize insight into and understanding of retarded communication stated with compassion but without pity. Retarded development is accepted as an unfortunate fact; the development of speech and language is the primary objective of the book; the methods are presented clearly and economically.

This book is timely. Its predecessor, *Teaching the Retarded Child to Talk*, has served well and contains much that is as useful as when first published, but new information and concepts about speech, language, and learning have become available and require dissemination. Every person who lives or works with retarded children will find this book to be both a ready reference and a systematic instructional guide to speech and language development.

PAUL MOORE
University of Florida,
Gainesville, Florida

Introduction

THIS REVISED EDITION of *Teaching the Retarded Child to Talk*, published in 1961, is almost a totally new book. We have learned so much in the past fourteen years, seen so many bright people become deeply involved in the education of children with special needs, that it is exciting to read the introduction to the 1961 edition and realize how much actually has happened.

We have experienced great changes in attitude and expectations. Our philosophy remains the same: every child should have a chance to realize his potential.

We use different words with many different meanings, we have more definite goals and systems for reaching these goals. We have many therapists specializing in the treatment of delayed communication skills, and many universities now have departments of special education cooperating with departments of speech and language.

This means that more help is available to parents and children.

Working with a young child with retarded development, helping his family to help him, and being a part of that thrill and joy that come with the first spoken word, are most rewarding experiences.

A severely retarded child very likely will never have perfect speech; but if he can make his wants known and communicate with those about him, he is doing very well. Many of our children learn to carry on fairly good conversations, using all or most of the parts of speech.

We honestly do not know of one developmentally retarded child who has no communication problem.

It may be his voice—too loud, too soft, too hoarse. It may be a problem of stuttering or faulty articulation. It may be a language problem—difficulty understanding the meaning and the true use of words, either single words or a combination of words.

Parents ask, "Isn't there anything I can do myself to help my child talk?" This question has been heard far too many times to go unheeded.

Many families live too far from trained help and also may find private lessons too costly over the long period required for success.

In the authors' own experience, this has always been a hard situation to accept.

It is now true that most speech and language clinics study all children brought to them. No longer are children refused evaluation, diagnosis, and therapy either in a clinic or by a therapist just because measurable IQ falls below the "slow learner" category. In 1961, very few clinicians or therapists had been trained to work with our children.

By "our" children, we mean children with seriously delayed development, severe learning disabilities, physical handicaps, such as cerebral palsy. Actually these children have more than one problem and could all be called multiply handicapped.

For many years, in textbooks about "speech correction" or language development, it has been said that Downs Syndrome (Mongoloid) children would never learn to talk, or if a child had an IQ under 50, very little speech could be expected, just naming and using single words, and since time was thought to mean nothing to these children, correct verbs would not be used. If time meant nothing, then why should the child use the words "did" or "will do"? These children have been referred to as "today" children, yesterday and tomorrow having no meaning.

Very likely these ideas came from observing children in institutions where they had been since baby days, in cribs. They had never had a chance to learn to play, to explore, to share, and the days were all alike. The children were kept clean (we hope), fed, and taken outdoors periodically (maybe, if they had learned to walk). It was in the early fifties when we began to realize that these children were able to do many things. Just because they never had a chance, it was said, "They can't."

In teaching any handicapped person to talk or communicate, the goal must be good, usable language.

With good, usable language the child should learn to:

1 Follow directions received by listening to spoken directions, understanding gestures and picking up signals.
2 Say own name or show name tag (ID) when asked, "What's your name?"
3 Make wants and feelings known.
4 Listen courteously while others talk.
5 Communicate own ideas and needs.
6 Say "Please," "Thank you," "You're welcome," "Excuse me," "Good-bye," "How are you?" "Fine, thank you," "I had a good time, thank you," "No, thank you."
7 Carry on a conversation with children own age.

8 Give and accept a compliment.

9 Greet and say "Goody-bye" to guests.

10 Call people by name.

11 Smile at people.

12 Use the telephone to call: the doctor, the fire department, the police department, a friend, and *get to the point.*

13 Accept and deliver a message.

14 Whisper, speak softly, control volume of voice.

15 Ask for help when needed.

16 Ask for directions as to which way to go.

17 Ask a good "wh" question (*What, where, who, when*).

18 Speak in simple sentences.

19 Give directions clearly and gently. To be a good helper, one must learn not to bark or shout orders but to speak gently when in authority. This is especially important when an older student is called upon to help with younger children in school.

20 Listen to stories and short poems and respond within context.

21 Take part in "pretend" or dramatic play, especially with puppets.

22 Listen to and follow directions (this is repeated from the first item—it cannot be overemphasized). Added to the task of following directions should be asking for help when needed to follow directions or to complete any task.

Not all children will succeed in this entire list of goals for useful language. Each step is a real achievement. The degree of success varies with each individual child with his own unique speech problem and ability at each period of his development. These achievements are listed to serve as guideposts to the steps to be traveled to communicate usefully with people. Communication is a social process.

This book is intended to help parents and teachers to work with children after some study and careful planning. Many very basic ideas must be learned and carefully studied so you can plan wisely and productively.

Trying too hard should be avoided, for with too much unwise or unknowing pushing ahead, frustrations and failure can spoil all your hard work, no matter how seriously you go about it. You owe it to your child to learn as much as you can about how speech and language develop *normally*, what can cause delays, and what you can do about it. Chapter 5 will tell you how you start to work with your child after you have learned the necessary basics.

How different things are now—and each day brings more exciting news about new ways being found to help our noticeably delayed children to move about so they can explore and learn about things, to listen and to talk or sign so they can communicate and play together, work together, sharing their lives, labor, and love as they receive the interest and love from others, and a feeling of worthwhileness.

1

Why Some Children Fail to Learn to Talk

THE PURPOSE OF THIS BOOK IS TO HELP parents and teachers of very young retarded children who have not started to talk or who talk very poorly.

In a clinic in a big-city hospital, of the first two thousand retarded children examined, almost one-third had been brought in because the parents said, "He doesn't talk."

So very often the first, and in fact the only, complaint parents make when they come to a speech clinic or a clinic for handicapped children is, "If he could only talk," or "If he could just start talking, I'm sure he would be all right." It is important for these parents to understand that learning to talk will help a child with retarded development to a happier, more useful life, but *just* learning to talk will not completely solve the problem.

Babies are expected to say their first word around their first birthday. If a child has not started to talk by his second birthday, it's time to look into the problem. By the third birthday much valuable time has been lost. There was a time when people would say, "He'll outgrow it." *There is always a reason why a child does not talk*, and it should be discovered as soon as possible.

That a child is developmentally delayed is often the main reason why he does not talk, but there are other reasons too. Children who do not talk when they can reasonably be expected to need careful study. There may be one or a combination of several causes for a child's not talking:

Why some children fail or are delayed in learning to talk

1 The child may have a sensory (input) problem.
    A This could be a partial or total hearing loss.
    B The child could be visually impaired or blind.
    C The child could have difficulty learning about the meaning of touch, pressure, or motion.
2 The child may have an emotional problem.
3 The child may have some damage, defects, or malformed parts of his mouth, very necessary for making the sounds that become words.
4 The child may have some damage in his brain.
    A Such damage interferes with understanding the messages coming into the brain.
    B The brain damage can interfere with attaching meaning to what is heard, seen, and touched.
    C The brain damage can interfere with selecting the right gesture, or word, to express an idea.
5 The child may be developmentally delayed and not mature enough to start to talk. The mental growth may be slower than the physical growth so he is mentally too young to understand and to speak as you would normally expect him to do.

The child may have more than one of these problems at the same time.

1. If your child is *deaf* you very likely can remember a change in the way he acted as a baby, especially if you have other children with whom to compare him. A deaf

child will stop cooing and making baby noises at about six months. A deaf baby's eyes are very active because he must use them to keep track of things. On the other hand, a deaf baby will probably start to walk at the same age that your other children did.

All children learn to listen before they learn to talk. If they have hearing problems that make it very hard for them to understand noises, sounds, and people, they have a hard time learning to say words. It's like trying to sing a tune played for you on a piano with some of the notes missing. Loss of hearing can be traced to any one of several causes. The safe and practical thing to do is to take your child to a doctor or a hearing clinic as soon as you suspect that his hearing is not perfect. Whatever the cause of deafness, these children can be helped to communicate, but they need professional aid and carefully planned help. There are good programs for hearing-impaired children and many places you can go for help.

If your baby does not see his world because he is *blind*, or sees it blurry or distorted (this is called visual impairment) he will very likely have some delay in learning to attach meaning to sound. We need to receive information not only through our ears but also from our eyes as well as from our total body through the feelings received from touch, pressure, and motion. The hearing-impaired baby must depend upon his eyes and his sense of touch, pressure, and motion to take in information. The visually-impaired child must depend upon his ears and his sense of touch, pressure, and motion to take in information.

Some children have damage to part of the brain that blocks or slows down receiving information from touch, pressure, or motion, or the understanding of the words that stand for touch, pressure, motion, or action. These children can learn to say "pencil" but do not understand that it means something to write with. A child normally sees a pencil, hears the word, and sees a pencil and hears it named at the same time, and without any conscious thought knows it is something to write with. When the channels that tell a child this are not working right, it is very difficult to comprehend the word "pencil" as a meaningful, useful sound symbol that means something to write with.

A blind or visually-impaired child will experience some delay in his baby days playing with sound because he does not pick up the happy or unhappy expression on his mother's or daddy's face, and he needs this feedback or reinforcement to know how he is getting across to his listeners.

The child who is having problems receiving messages from touch, pressure, or motion will likely have trouble attaching meaning to the very necessary words "wet" and "dry" and even the meaning of the pressure and/or discomforts of a filled diaper. Toilet training thus is delayed and very difficult.

2. If an *emotional* problem is keeping your child from talking, it is a very serious matter and you will need a great deal of help from someone who really knows how to handle such problems. *Very few children* fail to talk because of this kind of problem.

3. To produce the wide variety of combinations of sounds that become words, lips, tongue, jaw, teeth, gum ridges, palate, voice box, and the muscles for breathing must work together. This working together is called *articulation*. The parts of the speaking mechanism move so fast and automatically that we are not even aware of the movement unless we slow down sometimes to emphasize a word. When any part of the articulation mechanism is damaged or is slowed down, the output or utterance of words can become dis-

torted, some sounds substituted for other sounds or just left out of words, slurred, or endings clipped off of words. Downs Syndrome (Mongoloid) children usually have severe articulation problems because the tongue is seldom smooth and the roof of the mouth is unusually high.

Damage or slowing down of any one part of the entire system can cause trouble. Usually if one part is not working right, another part will be faulty also. Our tongues move at a tremendous speed to channel the air stream, to shape vowel sounds, to touch the teeth, or gum ridges. Lips move very fast to help shape sounds. All this movement is very fast. When development is delayed, very often the child will not have control of these necessary movements, and this results in no speech or very slow production of the sounds to make words. Many children so handicapped have early feeding problems because they have difficulty sucking and swallowing. Some of the sluggish movement can be the result of damage to parts of the brain, or elsewhere in the nervous system.

A cleft palate and/or cleft lips makes it very hard for a child to learn to eat and to talk. Surgery has done wonders for many children with this added problem, but it is not always possible to rebuild the cleft. A device called an *obturator* is sometimes fitted into the mouth. This is an artificial roof for the mouth that hitches onto the teeth very much like a partial denture. Some children cannot tolerate an obturator; for others it helps very well.

With a cleft palate condition, nerve endings in the mouth are often damaged so the child has still another difficulty in therapy because he cannot get the messages from the speech area of his brain to the parts of his mouth he is trying to learn to control. This problem is so complicated you should attempt lessons for saying words only with the guidance of an expert clinician. This does not mean you don't do anything. You should go ahead and do *all* the learning-to-listen activities, attaching meaning to sound, identifying objects, and pictures, learning to respond to "no," "don't touch," "come to me," and "sit down." (See Chapter 8.) And you can proceed to teach signing as soon as the child is ready. (See Chapter 14.)

The child with cerebral palsy also has a very complicated problem. Nerve damage causes the muscles for producing speech and rhythmic breathing, so necessary for talking, not to work properly. You should be guided by the advice of an expert in a clinic. But you can go ahead with learning to listen, attaching meaning to sound, identifying objects and pictures, and learning to respond to the words that are appropriate for his limitation. If the cerebral-palsied child can control his hands, he can learn to *sign*. Should hand control be a problem, then you will use still "another way" (see Chapter 14) and teach him to use a communication board.

4. Some children do not start to talk at the expected age because something has happened to damage the part of the brain that helps them to understand sounds, to store memories of experiences with sounds, and to say words. *Brain damage* like this can be caused before, during, or after birth. It can be caused by accidents. It can be caused by illness of the mother when she is carrying the baby. It can be caused by problems that develop during the birth or right after birth, such as the baby's not being able to breathe right away or having a problem that causes jaundice (turning yellow) in the first few days of life.

As far as anyone knows, brain damage is not inherited or passed on from either parent. Its effect is almost like a "stroke" that stops speech in an older person. It really isn't a stroke because it is not caused by the same thing but it acts almost the same way. Older people who lose their speech after a stroke can sometimes make their ideas known because they *did* have speech and can remember ideas. These ideas are stored away and help them to get along with people. A baby whose brain has been damaged never did have speech, so he has no "savings account" of stored-away ideas and experiences with sounds and words to draw from. He gets terribly upset because he can neither tell you what he is thinking nor understand what you are saying. Words are just more noises that have no meaning to him.

This kind of child may be a little late in walking. You will feel that something is wrong because no matter how you try, you can't get him to mind by talking to him. He is not really naughty or stubborn. He just doesn't understand what you say so he does not know what you expect him to do. His behavior goes from bad to worse and you will find yourself very upset and worn out trying to control him. Such a child is fighting the whole world, including himself, because he cannot understand it.

Finding out whether brain damage is the reason why a child does not talk is a task for specially trained clinicians called language pathologists. Many brain-damaged children can be taught to talk. But the parents must first learn how to manage the child and then they must work right along with the teacher.

5. If your child has not learned to talk by the time he is three years old, if you have not noticed any signs of deafness, and if his behavior has not been too bad, the chances are that your child is develop-mentally delayed. He may have a severe learning disability resulting in delays in

development. His mind is just not growing as fast as it was expected to grow. In this case, you should take your child to a good clinic where a psychologist will study him.

For example, let's say your child is four years old. If his mental age, as determined by standard tests given by a psychologist, is two years and your child is talking like a two-year-old, you can safely say that his delayed speech is due to retarded development. This could be from any one cause or combination of causes.

Now let's say this same child has *no* speech at all; *something else in addition* to retarded mental development is causing this delay in starting to talk. If a child has convulsions, or paralysis, or if he has something wrong that the parents can see (like missing fingers or "strange-looking" eyes), you will expect something else to be "wrong" too. But when a child looks all right and walks all right, and even if he starts to walk a little later than he should, parents are very slow to suspect trouble until speech is long overdue. The clinic's speech pathologist who studies your child can tell you if anything else is wrong and what you should expect.

There are some things you should avoid.

1. Don't let anyone but a good doctor tell you your child is "tongue-tied." *Very, very seldom* is a tongue "tied." A little bit of tissue called the *frenulum,* in the middle of the bottom side of the tongue, seems to anchor it. Once in a great while, this may be too short. But a child *will try to talk anyway.* He will have ideas and try to get them across. Your doctor can tell you what to do about this.

2. Don't rush to someone who claims to work wonders or guarantees speech in a few lessons. There is only one thing to do and that is go to a clinic where more than one person will study your child.

You can spend a lot of money going from one specialist to another. These people cannot get together to talk things over. That is why you should go to a clinic.

Where are these clinics? Most large cities have a special clinic for children in one of the large hospitals or in a special hospital for children.

If you do not live in or near a large city, write to or telephone your state medical society office (usually located in the state capital) and ask for information about a clinic for retarded children or a speech and hearing clinic. Or write to the National Association for Retarded Citizens (2709 Avenue E East, Arlington, Texas 76011) for a list of clinics. Big hospitals and universities also have speech and hearing clinics.

When you find out where the nearest clinic is, write or telephone for an appointment. Don't just pack up your child and go—you might find the clinic unable to see your child on that particular day and your trip will have been wasted. Ask for an appointment and when you get one keep it promptly. Bring your baby book if you have one, so you will have a record of your child's birth, weight, age of sitting up, etc.

Be sure to seek a clinic that will make a medical diagnosis and not just a language test. It is beyond the duty of anyone but a doctor *and* an expert experienced clinical psychologist to tell you that your child is developmentally retarded.

You must find a good reliable specialist or clinic. Trust these people to tell you the truth. Believe what they tell you. Don't shop around from one doctor to another hoping someone will say what you want to hear. In choosing a specialist or clinic, put trust in the information from your medical society.

There are many things that cause a child to be developmentally delayed or retarded. Some can be explained, many cannot. Often the doctor knows *how* these things happend but cannot always tell you *why* they happen. A good doctor can explain many things to you. Try to believe him and put your trust in him. If your doctor feels that you trust him and will cooperate with him, he can be a source of great strength to you and help you gain some peace of mind. If your attitude is one of doubt or even hostility, the doctor might very easily not put much effort into trying to help you because he feels you won't cooperate with him.

Someone on the clinic team can answer the nagging questions that come to your mind and can help you. Don't be afraid to ask direct questions.

If you do not understand what has happened to your child, you may go along feeling very guilty or very suspicious. If you feel this way, you cannot face the future with your child—you cannot plan wisely for him and you cannot help him.

You must know as much about your child as it is possible to know so you can live in peace and help him. *If you understand the problem, you can help him.* You MUST KNOW:

1 How fast he is going to progress and what goal you can set for him.
2 How much special help and planning he will need.
3 Where he is going to get the special help he will need.
4 What kind of school he needs and what you can expect when he becomes an adult.

After your clinic visits are over, write a letter to the clinic asking for a written report on their findings. This will give you a clear statement of the situation and be helpful to you if you must teach your child yourself or be helpful to his teachers in whatever special school he may attend.

It's a good idea at this point to start a special file to keep all records and reports about your child in good order for handy and quick reference.

2

Language and Speech

WHEN YOU NOTICE that your child isn't listening or talking as expected, and you seek help, you are introduced to an entirely new set of words that your physician or the specialists who study your child may use to explain to you why your child is not developing at a normal rate.

Your concern is that your child doesn't talk, and you may have been told that this is not just a speech problem but a *language* problem.

Speech and language are two very different words, and it is necessary to know the meaning of each so you will understand the goals that will be reasonable for your child. What is the difference, and what do these words, speech and language, mean?

Speech is the production of sounds put together in such a way that a certain meaning is intended to be understood by another person.

Language is a system for the putting together of meaningful sounds and movements, plus the hearing and understanding of sounds and movements; it is the entire give-

and-take of exchanging ideas by meaningful (symbolic) sounds, movements, and gestures.

Speech

Just saying words is not really speech. The spoken words must have meaning to the person who produces the words and carry meaning to the person or persons who hear them.

If a child does not attach meaning for his own use to what he hears, or does not produce a word that has real meaning to him, the problem is serious, and he will require a great deal of training to use words.

Words are "said" in hundreds of combinations that are made up not only of word-sounds, but also of melody, pitch, volume, and rhythm. Speech is good and pleasant when all these things work well together and convey an idea.

When a child is unable to say the sounds or syllables as they should be said, he has an *articulation* problem.

We must not worry about an articulation problem until ideas are being exchanged (received or given) comfortably. When a child is using words to express wants and feelings, is putting some words together, is making sentences, or is asking questions, then we can start to help with articulation so words can be understood by others more easily. Actually, the child has moved along to using language when he is doing all these things.

If you start right away to demand perfect articulation you might just turn him off. The child might react easily with—"If you don't like the way I say it, I just won't say it!" This must be avoided, so be patient and be willing to wait until your child is comfortable using words with you.

If the words are monotones, and have no variety or are spoken too high, too sharp, too husky, too hoarse, too nasal, or too soft, it is called a *voice* problem.

If the words come out jerkily instead of easily, it is called a *rhythm* problem. This problem may be so severe that it interferes with your child using speech without a great deal of effort. Stuttering is a severe rhythm problem.

All words have a purpose and a special meaning. The way we say them has meaning, too. Whether we say words pleasantly or gruffly, is up to us to decide. The *meaning* of words is decided by the "language" we speak and that is determined by where we live and where we grow up.

The production of words is determined by breathing, shifting tongue, lips, and jaw fast enough and with enough variety to put together the thousands of sounds we need to communicate with each other.

Our words are made up of vowels and consonants. The vowels are *a, e, i, o, u,* and sometimes *y.* All the rest of the sounds are consonants.

The vowels have many sounds. For instance, *a* sounds one way in "bat" and another way in "car" and another way in "ball." The differences in the sounds are made by the way you use your tongue and voice and sometimes your lips. Say *"ooh"*—your lips do most of the work. Say *"up"* and you will notice that your tongue is flat toward the back. Now say "it." Your tongue is working up toward the front. Say "cat" and your tongue works in the middle. This tongue action is hard for some children, especially for children with Downs Syndrome.

Teaching vowel sounds is not too hard after the first vowel sound is learned; new ones come easily.

Your lips, tongue, and palate working alone or together produce the consonant sounds. Say these words one at a time: "by," "this," "far," "very," "dog," "tie," "cut," "go," "hush," "see." You feel that your lips, tongue, and jaw are busy and shifting from one position to another in many combinations.

Many of our children have a hard time learning to control the movements necessary or to make the rapid shifts that keep a steady flow of sounds coming along.

You must hear yourself in order to know whether you are making the same word sounds that other people make. The deaf child doesn't talk because he has never heard a word-sound pattern. A child who is hard of hearing will leave out certain sounds because he does not hear them clearly enough to form his own word-sound patterns.

Many of our children may have no problem hearing the spoken words but do not notice the little differences that are so necessary for good articulation.

Children who lisp usually are not aware that they are lisping, because although they hear the words of others and also hear themselves produce a lisped sound, they are not aware of it. In other words, they don't seem to be able to listen and notice the difference between "this" and "thith."

Many children leave out, slur over, or confuse sounds because they do not hear the small differences between sounds like "bit" and "bet," "then" and "them," "pat" and "bat."

Language

Language is a very complex process which includes learning *to understand* the meaning of symbols, gestures, spoken words, and written words, and learning *to express* thoughts, ideas, and emotions through gestures, speech, and writing. In other words, language is a system of symbols that human beings use to communicate with one another. Speech or the spoken word is only one part of language. Speech is the spoken word—the manner in which we put sounds together that mean something (sound symbols) to form words. We then put words together to make meaningful sentences. This requires thought and planning.

Mynah birds say words, even sentences, but do not have language. Their words are not a part of a system requiring thought to make the sound symbols work for them to exchange ideas.

We all communicate by gestures, facial expression, tone of voice, stressing of certain words as we talk, and body stance.

Gestures are symbols. We point at something or move our hands in various ways and put an idea across. We frown and look cross—this is a symbol that we are not happy or pleased. We stand up straight and tighten up and look strong and tough. The tone of voice we use carries meaning. Just stressing certain words in a sentence can change the entire meaning of that sentence. All written material carries meaning only by a symbol system.

Symbols stand for something not necessarily present and/or touchable. We can't touch "happiness," but we can put the symbols of happiness on our faces, in gentle voices, soft touches, or relaxed attitudes.

Language is the using of a system of symbols that has meaning to a group of human beings.

To communicate with one another, we must learn to understand the meaning of all these symbols. No wonder that language learning or learning to communicate will be one of the most difficult tasks your child must master. It is very complex, very powerful, and very wonderful. Some great scientists have called the use of language "magical."

Before a child can use language, he must learn to:

1 Look, listen, and pay attention for increasingly longer periods of time.
2 Separate and know the difference between gestures and sounds that are meaningful and needed and those gestures and sounds that are not needed at that particular time. This means sorting out the gestures and sounds around him.
3 Attach meaning to gestures and words.
4 Use gestures and words to "tell" what he sees and hears.

If we agree that a child with retarded development takes a longer time to go through the stages of development than other children require, then we can understand why anything so complex as talking is much more delayed in a handicapped child than other learning skills.

For example, your child can be taught to walk (or move about in a walker or wheelchair), feed himself, be toilet trained, and play with things that he is able to handle such as inset puzzles, peg boards, and stringing beads. Learning these things depends upon being physically able and getting enough practice with help and careful guidance.

These activities are motor skills, with visual guidance—his eyes must help him plan his action. A great deal of thinking is not required. Once a child has learned to move about, or feed himself, he can do the same thing over and over again without thinking and planning each move. It is true there are many ways to move about: running, skipping, crawling, climbing, hopping—but once a child learns to walk or run, he will likely learn the other ways to move.

Thinking is always involved in language, and learning to think about what you want to "say" is not always easy.

The child with normal development begins very early to understand the meaning of sounds around him, tone of voice, gestures, pressures (like being held too tight or tensely), and facial expressions. He also learns to understand the speech of those around him; at as young as six months a baby can be quieted when someone talks gently to him. He will also stop crying when he hears the refrigerator door being opened or closed—if he is hungry—or the sound of bath water—if he is happy during his bath time.

At seven months a baby will raise his arms to be picked up when mother says, "Come." He is imitating her gestures, arms extended with hands palms up.

The toddler will respond when he is told, "Bring me the ball."

At the same time the child is learning to understand the world around him through hearing, seeing, tasting, smelling, moving, and exploring.

The first sound a baby makes is crying. He is experimenting very soon with his voice, moving his lips, tongue, and jaws.

When you were asked, "Did you hear him cry immediately after delivery?" it is a very important question. The birth cry is the beginning of the chain of events that must take place before the baby is ready to talk. If the birth cry is absent this may be one of the "soft signs" indicating that a baby's development should be watched very carefully for roadblocks during the growing years.

A baby learns very early to make connections between things and what they are for. He learns he can use his fist to bring a thing to his mouth. The "thing" might be his own fist that he puts into his mouth.

Later when given a spoon to play with, he will hammer it, then bring it to his mouth. If he is not interested in the spoon, he will likely pitch it away from him. After watching others around him use a spoon to carry something to the mouth, he will soon learn that that spoon is used to bring good things in life to his mouth. He has attached meaning to a spoon as a tool.

As the baby grows, mother learns quite suddenly that crying sounds are not all alike and mean different things. A hungry cry is a different cry from a cry of discomfort or fear or anger. This occurs as early as six weeks of age.

The cooing and babbling that starts at about three or four months of age are the necessary beginnings of vocalizing that will become meaningful and that will one fine day produce the beautiful sound "mama," and mother is elated because she knows it means *me*. (A detailed scale is included in Chapter 3 to give you a step-by-step picture of how language develops and emerges.)

A baby will attempt to imitate the single words he understands, single words that have taken on meaning for him. The speech-sound play that goes on between parent and child is the basis of speech. The parent imitates the sounds that a child makes and the child will often get a quizzical look on his face—as much as to say, "Where did you learn that?" Soon he attempts to imitate his parent as well as playing with the sounds that he himself makes. He blows little bubbles, repeats some sounds, stops, then repeats them again. He seems to be listening to himself, liking what he did, then does it over again. He is having fun with sound.

The first word a child uses may have many meanings. "Mama" may mean mother, grandma, or any friendly, full-grown female.

The child may ask a question by merely changing the inflection of the word; "Mama?" meaning "where is my mama," or a crying "Mama" may mean, "I hurt—help me."

Talking begins then by putting together the practice sounds that the child accidentally made very early in his life. This does not happen in a haphazard way but gradually through attempts to imitate the words that adults were using with him. Mothers of very young children usually use a very limited vocabulary while speaking to their children. Speech of the mother of a baby is very much simplified and shortened.

The next step in the development of language is the putting together of words according to certain rules or grammar to make sentences. The very young child should have the ability to:

Use speech sounds:	baba, dada, mama
Use words:	mama, ball, cup
Make up his own phrases:	"Mama go bye-bye"

It is important to realize that language skills begin with the easy or concrete—things that can be heard, seen, tasted, or felt, things you can have a picture of, and things that have real meaning for the child. This is true with the development of speech sounds also; the earliest speech sounds that the child can imitate and later make by himself include the "easy to see and make" sounds: *m, p, b*. All children produce the vowels as their first utterances. It is not expected that children will be able to make more difficult speech sounds such as *ch, r,* or *j* until they have learned the earlier sounds.

Let's put it all together again, just so you can keep a clear picture of how a child moves from that first precious word to using language and talking in sentences. It goes along like this:

1 The first word that has meaning.
2 Many words with whole single meanings. At this point, a word will mean only one thing. "Bed" means just his own bed, then the beds in the house. He has not yet learned that "bed" can mean flower bed, bed rock, etc. And "dog" is his dog only. The words he uses are very real and very close to his everyday life.
3 Action words: eat, ride, wash, want (wanna).
4 Two words together that start to make phrases take on added meaning like size—"big ball"—shape, color, or texture. He will be adding directional words, "Up, daddy," or action words, "Want milk." He may use action words before, or at the same time, he uses words such as size, shape, color, and texture.

When the child is putting some words together and talking with you he will likely drop some of the words you use for him to imitate. You might say, "Look at the big truck," and he will say, "Big truck" or "Look truck." This is fine and very natural. He is keeping the important part of his sentence, the noun and the verb and maybe the adjective, and this makes it easier for him to remember the *important* words.

Very soon he will begin to imitate you, but he will not omit some helping words. He will keep the words in the same order but will add "is," "will," "have," "had," "in," "on," "up," "he," "her," "it." He might not imitate you exactly—he will come close to it, though. Don't worry about it. He's doing fine at this stage.

The child might not follow all the good rules for grammar at this time, but he is adding more parts of speech, and the sentences are more like real sentences.

Finally the child will produce his own sentences without having to imitate you. He is dreaming it up himself. He will make up some words on his own that are very reasonable, but the English language is very confusing and difficult. He might say, "I *digged* a hole." Surely you didn't give him the word "digged," but just his using the word tells you he has learned the rule for adding *-ed* to tell something that has already happened. He is thinking about how to tell you something in sentences.

Don't try to correct every error in grammar. In time he will correct himself if you set a good example yourself. Keep him happy with his new skills!

3

How Children Learn to Talk

BEFORE YOU FIND OUT how to teach a child with retarded development to talk, you should know how a normal child learns.

A child learns to talk only after he has learned to listen and to understand what he hears. Words must have meaning to him before he feels the need to use them.

A child begins to listen in his baby days when he first turns his head to follow his mother's voice. It doesn't take a baby long to learn when his mother is cross and when she is happy. He'll start to cry if Mother or Daddy speaks gruffly. This crying is his "talking" in response to the message he receives and understands from the gruff voice. This isn't talking as we think of it, but it tells you that he doesn't like the sound of your voice.

A baby learns very early what sounds mean. If he enjoys his bath, he'll start to wriggle all over and smile and coo when he hears the water running in the bathtub. If he doesn't like his baths, he may cry.

Some babies will get excited when they hear the refrigerator door open, and it isn't long until they know the sound of Daddy's car. This is learning what sounds mean.

These things are the beginnings of living in a speaking world. The baby does not talk with words, but he lets you know he's in touch with you. His radar is working. He tells you with his whole body that he is reacting to you. He wriggles with joy. He stiffens up with anger. He might even throw himself on the floor and kick and hit in a tantrum to tell you with his whole body that he does not like what is happening.

Babies make a lot of noises; they coo, cluck, make sucking sounds, blow bubbles, and play with various sounds. This playing with sound is called *babbling*.

One day, when he is about a year old, one of these playful noises sounds like "mama."

Before a baby's first birthday he learns to imitate, to copy some simple little actions. He learns to wave bye-bye. He learns to patty-cake, and he learns to show you how big he is.

These baby acts are still ways of telling you his response with his whole body, but he is doing it now in a way set by someone else.

His wriggles for joy were his own ideas. Now he picks up an idea from someone else by *hearing* them say "bye-bye" and *seeing* them wave a hand.

The first time he waves "bye-bye" everyone smiles and laughs and tries to get him to do it again. It's so much fun that he does it again, and again, and again, and he has learned to do something.

It is the same story when he says "mama." He makes the sounds "ma-ma" quite by accident, but of course Mother thinks he called her and it makes her happy. The child responds to the mother's happiness by making the sounds again, and "mama" becomes a real word.

It is true all over the world that babies say "mama"

whether they are born in Borneo or Keokuk, Iowa. "Dada" happens the same way, but Daddy needs a little more imagination to hear it. (Most babies all over the world say "papa"!) These are the beginnings of language.

Children usually say first the words that begin with *b*, *p*, or *m*. Some examples of this are:

b: baby, bath, boy, bottle, bye-bye
p: potty, pipe, puppy
m: mama, more, milk

After the first word, others come along. "Na-na" for night-night. "Mu" for milk. "Dink" for drink. "Wa-wa" for water.

Putting "dink wa-wa" together won't come for a while, maybe not until a second birthday.

Little children don't say *l, r, th, h, wh, f, v,* or *s* for a long time. Trying to get a child to use a sound before he is ready just won't work.

There's a story about a mother being worried because her little girl couldn't say "lady." She said "waydy." Her mother worked hard to make this little girl say "lady." Finally the little girl got the idea that "waydy" was not the way to say it so she said "yady." And that's the way it goes. Children use *w* for *l* in many words, then use *y* before they can make the right sound for *l*.

Many of our words have sounds made of two letters that run together. These sounds are called blends. *Bl* as in "blow," *gr* as in "green," *cr* as in "crumb," *br* as in "brown," *gl* as in "glass," *tr* as in "train," and many others. Little children very often say a *w* sound for the *r* in "bread"; "twain" for "train"; or they may leave the second letter out altogether and say "g-een" for "green," "b-oo" for "blue."

When children don't move along to the next step but

keep on using these "first" sounds long after they are babies, especially after they are four years old, we call that "baby talk."

To review how children learn about sounds, we should remember this timetable:

Step 1 *Babies learn that sounds have meanings.* They learn that the look on a face and the pleasant or cross voice have meaning. They put things together in their own minds. They play with sounds.

Step 2 At about six or seven months of age *they learn that sounds have special meanings,* like Mother's voice, bath water, etc. They make more sounds themselves and *babble* along very happily.

Step 3 At about twelve or thirteen months *the first word is usually made.*

Step 4 *New words are added now and then* and for the next few months they will rattle along while playing, *using a lot of jargon* that sounds almost as if they were really talking. *They will often repeat or echo the last word of what they hear.*

Step 5 After eighteen months, children are off to a flying start to say words, and to put words together.

The following chart gives carefully detailed steps listing each development in proper sequence. You will note that what the child learns to *understand* (receptive language) is just a few jumps ahead of what he learns to say or convey (expressive language).

We are deeply indebted to Dr. Kenneth Bzoch and to Dr. Richard League for permission to include their scale for the emergence of language. This material is the basis for a system for evaluation developed by them, published under the title *Reel Scale: The Bzoch-League Receptive-Expressive Emergent Language Scale for the Measurement of Lan-*

guage Skills in Infancy.* The manual and test materials are available from The Tree of Life Press, Inc., 1309 North East 2nd Street, Gainesville, Florida 32601. For detailed scoring instructions and a listing of terms consult the manual.

AGE PERIODS

(Receptive Language) (Expressive Language)

ZERO TO ONE MONTH

(Receptive Language)	(Expressive Language)
Startle response to loud, sudden noises.	Frequent crying.
Activity arrested when approached by sound.	Begins random vocalizing other than crying.
Often quieted by a familiar, friendly voice.	Vowel-like sounds similar to "E" and "A" predominate.

ONE TO TWO MONTHS

Frequently gives direct attention to other voices.	Has a "special" cry for hunger.
Appears to listen to speaker.	Sometimes repeats the same syllable while cooing or babbling.
Often looks at speaker and responds by smiling.	Develops vocal signs of pleasure.

TWO TO THREE MONTHS

Responds to speech by looking directly at speaker's face.	Occasionally responds to sound stimulation or speech by vocalizing.
Regularly localizes speaker with eyes.	When played with, laughs and uses other vocal expressions of pleasure.

* © 1971 by Kenneth R. Bzoch and Richard League, reproduced here by permission of the authors.

Frequently watches lips and mouth of speaker.

Often vocalizes with two or more different syllables.

THREE TO FOUR MONTHS

Turns head deliberately toward the source of the voice.

Looks about in search of speaker.

Usually frightened or disturbed by angry voices.

Often laughs during play with objects.

Babbles (regularly repeats series of same sounds, especially when alone).

Often uses sounds like "P," "B," or "M."

FOUR TO FIVE MONTHS

Regularly localizes source of voice with accuracy.

Recognizes and responds to his (her) own name.

Usually stops crying when someone talks to him (her).

Uses vowel-like sounds similar to "O" and "U."

Expresses anger or displeasure by vocal patterns other than crying.

Usually stops babbling in response to vocal stimulation, but may occasionally continue babbling for a short time.

FIVE TO SIX MONTHS

Appears by facial and bodily gestures to be able to distinguish general meanings of (1) warning, (2) anger, and/or (3) friendly voice patterns.

Appears to recognize words like "daddy," "bye-bye," "mama," etc.

Takes the initiative in vocalizing and babbling directly at others.

Occasionally vocalizes with 4 or more different syllables at one time.

Stops or withdraws in response to "no" at least half of the time.

Plays at making sounds and noises while alone or with others.

SIX TO SEVEN MONTHS

Appears to recognize names of family members in connected speech, even when the person named is not in sight.

Responds with appropriate gestures to such words as "come," "up," "high," "bye-bye," etc.

Gives some attention to music or singing.

Begins some 2-syllable babbling (repeats combinations of 2 or more different sounds).

At least half of the time responds with vocalizations when called by name.

Uses some word-like vocal expressions (appears to be naming some things in his own "language").

SEVEN TO EIGHT MONTHS

Frequently appears to listen to whole conversations between others.

Regularly stops activity when his (her) name is called.

Appears to recognize the names of some common objects when their names are spoken.

Occasionally vocalizes in sentence-like utterances without using true words.

Plays speech-gestures games like "pat-a-cake" or "peek-a-boo."

Occasionally "sings along" with some familiar song or music without using true words.

EIGHT TO NINE MONTHS

Appears to understand some simple verbal requests.

Uses some gesture language (such as shaking head appropriately for "no," etc.).

Regularly stops activity in response to "no."

Will sustain interest for up to a full minute in looking at pictures if they are named.

Often mimics the sounds and number of syllables used in vocal stimulation by others.

Utterances now contain more consonants than at the 6-month stage.

NINE TO TEN MONTHS

Appears to enjoy listening to new words.

Generally able to listen to speech without being distracted by other sounds.

Often gives toys or other objects to a parent on verbal request.

Speaks first words often ("da-da," "ma-ma," "bye-bye," or the name of a pet or a toy).

Uses some exclamations like "oh-oh."

Often uses jargon (short sentence-like utterances of 4 or more syllables without true words).

TEN TO ELEVEN MONTHS

Occasionally follows simple commands like "Put that down."

Appears to understand simple questions like "Where is the ball?"

Responds to rhythmic music by bodily or hand movements in approximate time to the music.

Usually vocalizes in varied jargon patterns while playing alone.

Initiates speech-gestures games like "pat-a-cake" or "peek-a-boo."

Occasionally tries to imitate new words.

ELEVEN TO TWELVE MONTHS

Demonstrates understanding by responding with appro-

Uses 3 or more words with some consistency.

priate gestures to several kinds of verbal requests.

Generally shows intense attention and response to speech over prolonged periods of time.

Demonstrates understanding by making appropriate verbal responses to some requests (for example, "Say bye-bye").

"Talks" to toys and people throughout the day using long verbal patterns.

Frequently responds to songs or rhymes by vocalizing.

TWELVE TO FOURTEEN MONTHS

Appears to understand some new words each week.

Seems to understand the psychological feeling and shades of meaning of most speakers.

Will sustain interest for 2 or more minutes in looking at pictures if they are named.

Uses 5 or more true words with some consistency.

Attempts to obtain desired objects by using voice in conjunction with pointing and gesturing.

Some true words now occur in jargon utterances.

FOURTEEN TO SIXTEEN MONTHS

Demonstrates understanding by carrying out verbal request to select and bring some familiar object from another room.

Recognizes and identifies many objects or pictures of objects when they are named.

Consistently uses 7 or more true words.

More frequent use of consonants like *t*, *d*, *w*, *n*, and *h*.

Clearly recognizes names of various parts of the body (such as hair, mouth, ears, hands, etc.).

Most communication is now accomplished by using some true words along with gestures.

SIXTEEN TO EIGHTEEN MONTHS

Comprehends simple questions and carries out two consecutive directions with a ball or other objects.

Remembers and associates new words by categories (such as foods, clothing, animals, etc.).

From a single request identifies 2 or more familiar objects from a group of 4 or more familiar objects.

Begins using words rather than gestures to express wants and needs.

Begins repeating words overheard in conversation.

Evidences a continual but gradual increase in speaking vocabulary.

EIGHTEEN TO TWENTY MONTHS

Upon verbal request points to several parts of the body and various items of clothing shown in large pictures.

Demonstrates understanding by appropriate responses to such action words (verb forms) as "sit down," "come here," "stop that," etc.

Demonstrates understanding of distinctions in personal pronouns (such as "give it to her," "give it to me," etc.).

Imitates some 2-word and 3-word sentences.

Imitates environmental sounds (such as motors, animals, etc.) during play.

Has a speaking vocabulary of at least 10 to 20 words.

TWENTY TO TWENTY-TWO MONTHS

Follows a series of 2 or 3 very simple but related commands.

Recognizes new words daily at an ever increasing rate.

Recognizes and identifies almost all common objects and pictures of common objects when they are named.

Begins combining words into simple sentences (like "go bye-bye," "daddy come," etc.).

Speaks more and more new words each week.

Attempts to tell about experiences using a combination of jargon and some true words.

TWENTY-TWO TO TWENTY-FOUR MONTHS

Upon verbal request selects an item from a group of 5 or more varied items (such as comb, spoon, etc.).

Appears to listen to meaning and reason of language utterances, not just words or sounds.

Understands most complex sentences (for example, "When we get to the store, I'll buy you an ice cream cone.").

Occasionally uses 3-word sentences (such as "There it is," "Play with blocks," etc.).

Refers to self by using his (her) own name.

Begins using some pronouns but makes errors in syntax.

TWENTY-FOUR TO TWENTY-SEVEN MONTHS

Demonstrates an understanding of several action words (verb forms) by selecting appropriate pictures (for example, correctly chooses

Usually uses 2-word or 3-word sentences.

which picture shows eat-
ing).

When asked, points to smaller parts of the body (such as chin, elbow, eyebrow, etc.).

Recognizes and identifies general family name categories (such as baby, grandma, mother, etc.).

Often uses personal pronouns correctly (I, you, he, it, me, etc.).

Asks for help with some personal needs (such as washing hands, going to the toilet, etc.).

TWENTY-SEVEN TO THIRTY MONTHS

Demonstrates an understanding of word association through functional identification (correctly answers such questions as "What do you eat with?" "What do you wear?" etc.).

Understands size differences (correctly selects "the little doll," "the small book," "the large bowl," etc. from among a group of similar objects).

Recognizes the names and pictures of most common objects.

Names at least one color correctly.

Refers to self by using a pronoun rather than by his (her) proper name.

Repeats two or more numbers correctly.

THIRTY TO THIRTY-THREE MONTHS

Demonstrates an understanding of all common verbs.

Understands very long and complex sentences.

Tells gender when asked, "Are you a boy or a girl?"

Names and talks about what he (she) has scribbled or drawn when asked.

Demonstrates an understanding of most common adjectives.

Gives both first and last name when asked.

THIRTY-THREE TO THIRTY-SIX MONTHS

Shows interest in explanations of "why" things are and "how" things function.

Carries out three simple verbal commands given in one long utterance.

Demonstrates an understanding of prepositions (such as on, under, front, behind, etc.).

Regularly relates experiences from the recent past (what happened while he (she) was "out" or separated from parent).

Uses several verb forms correctly in relating what is going on in action pictures.

Uses some plural forms correctly in speech.

As you study this scale that tells you each important step a child must go through in developing a communication skill, you might wonder why it stops at the third birthday. In a normally developing child, this is the way it goes, and by the time the third birthday comes along, all the *basic* skills have been learned. As the child grows older, his use of speech and language becomes broader, he adds many words, and manages his sentence structure to better use in expressing his ideas, but the rules that tell us how to put words together are used automatically by the third birthday. The authors of this scale explain this in these words: ". . . beyond the third year may be likened to the completion of a painting by the artist after he has the basic configuration of the painting already well defined. The finishing touches may continue as a process that lends character and depth to the achievement, but the earlier structures remain as the foundation of the entire creation."

The hope is that your child will be in a nursery school program by the time that third birthday comes around. And you must remember that your developmentally delayed child at three years of age could still be not talking. Many handicapped children move along fairly well in receptive language (hearing and listening) yet lag a year or more in expressive language (saying and doing). This is why learning to listen is so very important for our developmentally delayed children. Hearing and listening must come first.

4

How a Child with Retarded Development Learns about Sounds and Words

WE HAVE SEEN how a normal child learns to communicate, how he comes to understand what sounds mean and how he learns to express his own ideas. You might think that a child with retarded development would follow the same pattern but follow it more slowly. This is not the way it goes. The steps are different for this special child.

Many babies diagnosed in infancy as retarded have trouble nursing—learning to suck and to swallow. Later on, these babies have difficulty in chewing and swallowing solid foods. This is because the "machinery" for eating—lips, tongue, jaw, palate—does not work properly. This same "machinery" is needed for talking. If the child has eating problems because of this, he will probably have trouble using his lips, tongue, jaw, and palate in learning to talk.

The cooing, babbling sounds a baby makes are learning experiences for a normal child. A handicapped baby does not make the same sounds. His are made only with difficulty and are less playful. Some handicapped babies don't make any cooing sounds. They don't seem to experiment with sounds as normal babies do.

When a baby coos, blows little bubbles on his lips, or babbles, a mother will usually "coo" back to the child, she will play with him. This give-and-take between mother and baby is very important in helping the child understand he is in contact with a person who gives him comfort and security.

Many babies, particularly babies with Downs Syndrome, are "too good." They lie quietly in their cribs, they don't cry for attention. Because of this, often they are not played with as much as a more demanding baby would be.

In such cases mothers usually feel, even if they have not already been told, that something is wrong. The deep fear that goes with this knowledge clouds the playful attitudes a mother must show toward any baby. All babies need to be played with.

On the other hand, a developmentally delayed baby, instead of being "too good," can be so extremely restless, hyperactive, and difficult to care for that the exhausted mother and baby never have a chance to "play." This kind of baby seldom is in repose long enough to be played with or to experiment with sounds.

In between the "too good" and "too restless" kinds of babies there are many handicapped babies who do play with sounds, but they do it later than normal babies and they do it differently. The sounds they make don't seem to build the foundation needed for speech.

Quite often a child with retarded development will say "mama" for a while and then not say anything for two or three years.

A normal baby will begin to use jargon when he is about a year old and will continue to do so for about six months. Many children with retarded development go through this jargon stage; children with Downs Syndrome may, although at a later age. (See Chapter 15.)

In this same six-month period, normal children begin to echo words they hear. It is their way of learning to speak a word. This phase is known as echolalia and in normal children it lasts only a short time. But some handicapped children, who may enter this phase at about the same time as normal children, may continue to echo words for much longer than six months. They will repeat almost any word, using the same tone of voice and very good articulation, but only after they hear the word spoken. If you say to such a child, "How are you?" he will not answer you; he will repeat after you, "How are you?"

For a child with echolalia, the words he says have no meaning. To teach him to talk you will have to pretend that he cannot make the word-sounds he echoes. You will have to teach him to attach meaning to sound just as if he had never said a word.

Even more important than how a child starts to make sounds is how he learns to understand them.

Many children with retarded development scream and cry when the vacuum cleaner is turned on. They stiffen with fear when the telephone or doorbell rings. Sirens terrify them. These fears are because the child does not understand that these sounds are not going to hurt him. A certain sign that this is what is wrong is when the child clamps his hands over his ears and either shuts his eyes tight or looks at you with a frightened look in his eyes.

We learn to recognize different sirens and although a siren bleating behind our car, or at a highway intersection, might frighten us momentarily, we process the shrieking noise and adjust to it. If you had not learned to attach meaning to these different sirens, you can imagine how terrifying they might be.

Some children with severe learning disabilities put their hands over their ears when a record player, radio, TV, or any flooding sound suddenly fills the air. The humming noise of a large crowd is very disturbing to many of our children. Some children completely ignore these usual household noises, although many of them are truly frightened.

Normal children accept these noises rather easily. They learn quickly that the vacuum is controlled by Mother, that the doorbell or telephone means no harm.

The failure to attach meaning to sound becomes very serious when a child is old enough to be expected to show respect for his own safety, the safety of others, and conform with the routine requirements of daily life. Children must learn very early certain limitations for their own safety. We teach these limitations by saying "stop," "no," "don't touch."

Teach the child the clear meaning of these simple words (see Chapter 8). Do not shower him with a torrent of words that he cannot understand. He will obey a short, simple order if he knows what it means. Instead of saying, "Now, Tommy, you know Mama doesn't want you to do that," say "No." However irritated you may be, remember that if you speak to the child in words he doesn't understand, he will be bewildered and frustrated and his behavior will go from bad to worse.

When your child does not respond to a command and *real danger* is involved, be very sure that he has understood it before you spank him. A spanking is all right when you are sure the child has understood you and has willfully disobeyed. But to the child who didn't know what you wanted him to do it is a sad shock that jolts the security your understanding and care have given him.

A word more about spanking. Spanking or hand slapping should be used *only* when there is real danger of an accident or injury to the child or someone else: running across the street or alley; reaching or grabbing something on the stove; grabbing at eyeglasses; or grabbing at you when you are driving the car; standing up in the car when it is moving. If you reserve spanking for such very serious risks only, you can be sure it will be meaningful. It also helps you to be relieved of the fright of an almost tragic happening. If you spank or slap for every little annoyance, your child will just scream in protest and not learn the seriousness of the real risky disobedience. You must not spank or slap the first time a child does a high-risk thing. He must be told and told carefully that he must not run across the street—tell him why—and make a big story out of getting *hurt*—and hurt real bad—blood and everything. *Then* if he goes ahead and repeats the risk, time to lay down the hand as you lay down the law. After the spank—and be sure you have spanked immediately—don't wait or he'll forget what he did, and you've wasted your energy and his learning experience. When the tears are dried, love him and tell him you love him very much and don't want him to get hurt.

Slap only hands that are making a fast and dangerous grab. Slapping a face is a very degrading and useless thing to do. His face didn't do anything—his hands did though! Striking a child for any little thing just teaches the child that hitting someone is O.K., and he'll try it on someone else. Always be sure your child knows why he has been spanked or why his hand has been slapped.

For the child's protection it is of utmost importance that

families and teachers learn to use one-word commands and teach the meaning of these important words.

We know now that babies with developmental delays do not learn to listen and attach meaning to sound the same way normal babies do. We know, too, that before children can be taught to talk, they must be taught to listen. Learning to listen may take as long as two years and it must be done carefully, step by step. The child must learn that one sound is different from another. Sounds have meanings and words have meanings. The meaning of these sounds tells him to do something.

At first the child will learn to "do" what the sound says with his whole body: rock a doll, clap his hands, walk, run, tiptoe. Later the sounds become word-sounds, and he will learn to attach them to the real things that they mean. The sound of "ball" means that round thing you play with. Patience is needed. Remember, it may take as long as two years to learn enough about attaching meaning to sounds and words before "saying" words can start.

When these word-sounds take on meaning, it is then time to start to *say* words. This means that the child *says* words when prompted to do so. The words he *says* take on meaning to him and gradually become *useful* to him.

As words—just names of things at first—become useful, the child will begin on his own to use words purposefully, and then he is really *talking*.

The goal for all children with developmental delay is *good, usable* speech. These children should progress through all the steps toward good, usable speech.

Children classified according to the American Association on Mental Deficiency as "Moderately Retarded" should progress through all the steps toward good, usable speech or good use of *signing* (total communication). (See Chapter

14.) Many will have trouble with some sounds that are hard to make. Many children with no other handicap often have trouble with *l, r, s,* and *th.*

Most educable children can learn to talk very well, although some will do better than others. The more educable child will use more words, make better sentences, and have fewer problems with sounds. In fact, many educable children have no speech problem at all except a delayed start. Others will need a lot of help to learn to speak well.

Speech correction—that is, correction of a problem in making sounds properly—can help, but it should not be attempted until the child has learned to communicate in spite of the defect. Correction of speech defects should not be allowed to interfere with comfortable language usage. Parents and teachers of children with retarded development should be careful not to draw attention to a speech defect unless they are reasonably sure that it can be overcome. We are more concerned about language development than just the correction of articulation (speech-sound problems).

5

So You're Going to Teach Your Child Yourself

YOU CAN BEGIN TO TEACH your child with planned, set-time lessons when he is about three year old. *But*—this does not mean you are not working with him from the time you first learn that your child's development is delayed or a disability is recognized.

Working and planned playing with your baby is called *infant stimulation* or *early intervention*. Some people and clinics regard *early intervention* as any planned program that starts before the child enters a school, either a "preschool" program or a day care program. Infant stimulation means anything you do with an infant that is planned and has a definite purpose to guide the baby, to stimulate and motivate him, to try new things and to explore and investigate things about him. It also means, and this is very important, that you are doing some fascinating things, and you are being a very interesting, loving person.

Start to communicate with your baby the very first time you hold him in your arms. Don't clutch him too tightly—hold him gently but firmly—snuggle him up to you—nuzzle his neck (that's fun for both of you!)—and talk to him. Your talk can be little nonsense sounds strung together or even sung together. Hum to him, let him hear your voice, let him see your face—and you had better be smiling—and let him feel the security of your arms and gentle firmness.

A good old-fashioned rocking chair is relaxing for both mama—or daddy—and your baby. The slow rhythm of movement is comforting. Did you ever rock a baby to sleep in front of a mirror and watch the old sandman take over? It's a beautiful experience, and you will almost fall asleep yourself.

You know, all this gentle security rubs off on you. You may be exhausted and about to collapse in that rocking chair, but in only a few minutes you'll find yourself relaxing. It will take a little practice on your part, but you can do it.

Talk a lot during bath time. Hold your baby to feed him, and let him hear your voice, soft and pleasant.

At about four to six months start to name parts of the child's body—nose, eyes, ears, hands, tummy, toes—while bathing or drying after a bath. Name clothing and body parts while dressing or undressing your baby. Name the different foods as you feed him. Make naming things a habit.

By the time your child can sit for planned lessons for about five minutes, he should be looking at you—looking into your eyes when you talk to him, even if you need to call his name first to get his attention and maybe make some silly sound to get him to look at you. It is very necessary that eye contact be established. Smile when your eyes meet.

He should be paying attention to your antics and to some favorite toy that he can hold by himself.

Reward Training

We all like to think we have done the right thing when we do anything. Any mother feels good when a meal is praised and every person feels good when a smile, a pat, a hug, tells him he has done something pleasing and appropriate. These actions are called *social rewards*.

Salesmen win trips to exciting places for successful salesmanship. When less able children respond to whatever task is being required, a food reward is given. This should be just a tiny bit of something he likes very much and should be popped into his mouth just as soon as possible when the right move has been made. You must quickly say, "Good work" or "Good boy" or "Good thinking" to fill those few seconds between his successful response and the food reward. These actions are called *tangible rewards*. You want to move to social rewards, away from food rewards, as soon as you feel the child has learned the task and can respond comfortably.

This is called *reward training*—giving a reward, whether it is a tiny bit of food, a special toy to hold, a smile, words, or real prizes, when the response, or even a move toward the hoped-for response, is obvious.

It goes like this:

```
┌─────────────────────────────┐
│ Ask child to do something   │
│    (stimulus)               │
│        ┌─────────────────────────────┐
└────────│ Child does it or starts to do it │
         │    (response)               │
         │        ┌─────────────────────────────┐
         └────────│ Reward                      │
                  │    (reinforcement)          │
                  └─────────────────────────────┘
```

The reward reinforces the feeling of success and the appropriate response becomes a working part of the child's behavior.

You are starting out on a long, tedious, but very happy job. That is, it will be happy if you make it so. You must be very patient, very careful, and very willing to try again and again. You must never let your child know that you have any doubts about his success from lesson to lesson. You will be happy beyond belief when that precious first real word comes.

Three plans must be followed at the same time:

1 Lip, tongue, and chewing exercises to get the machinery for speaking in usable condition.
2 Experiences in learning to *listen.* This is done with familiar and "fun" *sounds* first, then by listening to *words.*
3 Your retarded child *must* learn what "no," "don't touch," "come here," "hot," "sit down," mean as soon as you possibly can teach him. *This is for his protection.*

All three of these very important skills will be talked about in the next three chapters. Just remember—teach all *three* at the same time.

Here are some plans you must make for the lessons:

1 Set·a definite time each day for a lesson. Mark your calendar each day to be sure you don't skip a lesson.
2 Put all the things you need in a box or basket. Don't let anyone play with these things. Keep them for lessons only.
3 Choose a time when no one is around. If you can't find time to be alone with your child, go into the kitchen or bedroom and close the door. You must be very special to your child at this time. You will be surprised how important this time will be for your child when he knows you are his, all to himself, and he will look forward to having fun with you. *Don't let anyone interrupt*

you. Be very firm with the rest of your family. Be sure of their cooperation.

4 Lessons must be fun—let the child know that you enjoy them by smiling and laughing with him. Show him that you appreciate him and really want to spend this time with him. Never act as if you want to "get this over with."

5 Don't lose patience or get cross or feel that "all is lost."

6 Time yourself and don't work more than five minutes, no matter how well things are going. Two lessons a day for five minutes each is a good plan.

7 After about three months you can work a few minutes longer, slowly increasing the time to twelve or fifteen minutes, but never longer. It is much better to have two short lessons each day than one long one.

8 Tell the family what you are doing and ask them to help by seeing that you have the time free and quiet.

9 Turn off the radio or television. You cannot compete with it during lessons. Don't order the family to turn off the TV. Ask them to.

10 If your child has Downs Syndrome you may have one of his brothers or sisters close to his age work with you. You must, however, tell the other child to do exactly what you tell him to. Children with Downs Syndrome are born mimics, especially of children close to their own size. Other children will do better with mother alone for their first lessons.

11 Plan your lessons—know what you are going to do each day before you start. Keep a daily journal of what *you did*, how well it worked, and how the child responded. Do not skip a day. Keep your record up to date. This is very important.

12 Assemble all the material you are going to use for a lesson so that you don't have to interrupt it to go and get something. Once you capture your child's attention you must not distract him.

13 Work at a table that is clear of all objects except those you want him to see.

14 Don't use a patterned cover on the table. If your only usable table is covered too gaily, get a piece of *plain pale-colored* covering—a soft blue is good—and use it when you are having a lesson.

15 Don't wear a jingly or clangy bracelet during lessons. The child would rather look at the bracelet than listen to you.

16 If possible, use child-size chairs and table. You may be a bit creaky when you get up from the low chair, but your child will be more at ease in something of his own size, and he is the important member of the team. Sit on the floor if you have to but don't put a little child on a chair so big that his chin barely comes to the top of the table. A high chair or junior chair is fine. Don't tower over the child; be sure you are always on the same eye level with him.

17 Talking is a sociable business, and when your child has learned to listen, it would be helpful to have another child sit in on the lessons, if, of course, you can count on his cooperation. Individual lessons are necessary at the beginning and at times later on for special help; but after the very careful and challenging period of learning to listen, the rest of these lessons can well be done in a very small group.

18 Discipline yourself and your family to use *one-word* commands kindly, to be careful about floods of words, and never be impatient with the child's attempts to respond. Any attempt is a gain; love him and reward him for the attempt and he'll try harder next time.

19 Always remember to reward your child for every success no matter how small the success might be.

6

Exercise, Exercise

IT IS NOT UNCOMMON for a mother of a young handicapped child to report, "He was a very slow eater," or "It often took me an hour to get him to drink his milk." Four- and five-year-old children are often still on baby foods because they have so much difficulty eating. Sucking, swallowing, and chewing a baby usually learns automatically, but can be seriously delayed in a handicapped child. The same movements used in getting nourishment are the basic movements used to shape the sounds that make up words. To control sound making, the lips, tongue, jaws, and sound-producing mechanism (voice box or larynx) must be working together.

Another delayed activity for many children with retarded development is the making of sounds (cooing and babbling) that goes on very early in a baby's life. The "practice period" required for the making of speech sounds is often delayed or even missing in the development of a handicapped child.

You may need to work with your child to teach him to use his lips, tongue, and jaws. This includes learning to suck, to chew, and to swallow. Later you will need to encourage him to use the same parts to make sounds.

Be sure to make it a game that he will enjoy; but follow the rules: don't work more than five minutes at first, no matter how much fun you are having.

Lip Exercises

Learning to blow is the first lip exercise. You really don't exercise the lips alone, because blowing makes the tongue move a little bit too. The back part of the tongue flattens out to let the air go through in a controlled way.

Use a bright-colored feather about three or four inches long tied to a piece of yarn. The softer the feather, the better. (You can buy feathers in craft supply shops.) If you can't get a feather, use small torn bits of colored tissue paper. Show the feather to the child, let him touch it, and talk about how soft it is. Hold it up high and let it drift down to your lap. Have a little fun with it.

Then hold it in front of your mouth and blow it. Make a big show of blowing it. Then hold it near the child's mouth. Say, "Blow," and keep your lips in the blowing position. Do it again if he doesn't try. If he still does not try, keep the feather near his mouth, put your finger gently on his upper lip and say, "Blow." As you say it, the feather will move a little. If he still does not do it, toss the feather around a bit, let him enjoy watching it, then put it away and try again later. Blowing can be very hard for a cerebral-palsied child or a cleft-palate child to do.

It is harder to blow a horn or a whistle, but once in a while a child can do it before he can learn to blow a feather or to blow out a candle.

Get a fat sipper straw, the kind used with milkshakes,

and cut it into halves so it won't be too long. Give him one half, and you keep the other. Try blowing through this straw. Aim at the feather on the table in front of you. If he is still not blowing, you can try another way. Get the cardboard tube from a roll of toilet tissue or paper towels. Hold it to your mouth and blow at the feather. You can make a little noise. Say, "Boo!" if you want to. Show some surprise when the feather moves. Give another tube to the child and try the same thing again.

Learning to blow is the first step for learning to suck through a straw.

You might not need all this to teach the child to blow. Most children get the idea by watching you, but these extra ways will help if you don't have good luck the first way.

You may need to try the game "Give me a big kiss" to get those lips to pull in tight. Little girls like to have some lipstick on their lips and "kiss" a piece of paper or a hand mirror. All this helps a child get the idea of moving his lips into a "pucker."

Blowing out a candle is a good exercise. Be very sure to use a stout candle in a good holder that won't tip over easily. The warming candles used under casseroles, or vigil lights work out very well. Blowing out a cigarette lighter is a little harder, but it's an exercise that daddy can do with the child every now and then.

Of course, the excitement of blowing out a birthday candle is great.

"Peek-a-boo" is a helpful game and will be fun for the child. As he forms the last syllable ("boo") his lips will be in the blowing position.

Note this very carefully: if you have trouble with blowing and none of the exercises seem to work, skip them for a while and go ahead to the tongue exercises. Play with the feather every now and then—it's fun—and the child might just get the idea all of a sudden.

Tongue Exercises

If your child will lick an ice cream cone or a lollipop, you are in luck. If not, you will need to teach him. Licking is a very important step in gaining tongue control.

Many children with retarded development allow their tongues to hang out of the mouth. These children usually are droolers, because they don't use their tongues "automatically" to control and to swallow saliva. It is very messy and very distressing for all concerned.

Tongue movements necessary to suck are different from those used for moving food about in your mouth when you chew. All developing children move their tongues forward in order to suck milk from a nipple. However, if this forward movement persists after a child has learned to chew food, a problem referred to as "tongue thrust" can persist. Eating problems, dental problems, as well as speech problems may arise because of an extended period of tongue thrust.

A word of caution. Tongue thrust does not prevent your child from learning to speak. A tongue thrust may affect clear articulation, resulting in a lisp or other articulation problems. However, if your child has no speech, do not worry about a tongue thrust. If he or she is speaking, and you or your dentist suspects a tongue thrust, consult a qualified speech and language clinician before you begin any treatment (see reference for American Speech and Hearing Association).

Just learning to smile will pull the tongue in. Try it on

yourself and see if you can stick your tongue out and smile at the same time! Teach the child to imitate your smile as you look into a mirror together. Be a big ham. A hand puppet with an exaggerated smile painted on or a mouth you can move with your hand will often draw a smile from a child who doesn't go along with your smile. Keep trying; the "smile route" is the easiest and also teaches the child to have a ready smile, besides the bonus of keeping his tongue in his mouth.

Sometimes the tongue will pull back in the mouth with a *gentle* flick of your finger on the child's tongue. Be very sure you reward him if the tongue pulls in. We'll talk more about controlling drooling when we talk about sucking and swallowing exercises.

Now we are going to concentrate on tongue control. The child must learn to lift up or drop down the tip of his tongue, touching his upper or lower lip, and placing the tongue tip against his upper teeth or lower teeth. He needs these motions to make certain sounds. Check yourself to find out what your tongue does as you make each of these sounds: *th, ch, l, j, n, s, z.*

Moving the tongue sideways is necessary for controlling food in the mouth. So we'll start to "teach" the tip of the tongue to lick.

Use something you know he likes very well. It must be something sticky, a lollipop if he likes it, a little cake frosting stuck on the end of a spoon or on your finger, a little peanut butter, a tasty bit of gravy, anything you know he likes. (If you are using a lollipop, don't let him bite it, or keep it on his tongue to melt—he must lick it—you hold it.)

If he wants to hold the lollipop or spoon himself, that's all right, but be sure he stays on the job. You might need a second lollipop or spoon to work on yourself to show him how.

After a few good licks, reward him with a good lingering taste. Do not do this more than twice during a lesson.

He may twist his tongue in all directions to get the good stuff off the spoon. That is fine—he is working his tongue.

When you feel he is licking quite well, it is time to start learning to make the tongue go the way you want it to go.

Put a little sticky stuff on his lower lip, right in the middle. Have him lick it off. You should do it yourself first to show him how. Do this two or three times in a lesson.

When he can do this, put the sticky stuff near the corner of his lips, on the *outside* of the mouth, then do the same thing on the other side. Do this twice or three times during a lesson. When he can move his tongue tip to either side, and downward, then put the "bait" on the *outside* of the upper lip. The child must be able to do all these exercises before the next step.

If these exercises aren't working too well, here's another way to try. Get a sheet of lucite about 5″ x 8″ and have an oval shaped hole about 1½″ wide and ¾″ high cut *and smoothed* in the middle of the sheet. Let the child poke his finger through the hole. Now sit in front of a mirror so the child can see himself. A make-up mirror on a stand will do very well. Stick your tongue through the hole and wiggle it around. Have fun doing it. Now wipe it off carefully (keep that tissue box handy) and tell the child, "Now you do it —look here"—and point to the mirror. You hold the shield for him if necessary. As soon as he sticks his tongue through the hole reward him.

Now you can put some gooey stuff on the side of the shield away from him, and he must stick his tongue through the hole and work to get the reward, which is the good-tasting stuff on the shield. He should watch himself in the mirror set at least a foot away from the shield. Be sure to keep the shield wiped clean after each attempt. This can get a little messy; but it will work, and it's just as much fun as you make it. Vary the goodies—jelly, peanut butter, cheese, frosting, caramel, catsup, whatever you know he likes.

Now it is time to start exercising the tongue *inside* the mouth. Use a *tiny* bit of sticky caramel or peanut butter. Push it, with your finger, behind his upper front teeth, right in the middle. He must get it off with the tip of his tongue.

This won't be too hard because by now he has had fun doing the out-of-the-mouth exercises. He knows he has made you very happy because you gave him a big smile and lots of love after each try and each lesson.

When he can loosen sticky stuff from behind his teeth, put a tiny bit on the roof of his mouth, right behind the gums. Be sure it is tiny because he must not get frightened, or gag. Try this on yourself and see what happens to your tongue.

Your child is really making progress when he has learned all these tongue-tip exercises.

Sucking through a straw makes the tongue work way back in the mouth. To teach your child to do this use a clear plastic straw—a fat one. Cut it into two pieces. Using a short straw gets the fluid into the mouth quicker. Using a clear plastic straw allows the child to see the fluid move inside the straw. (If you have difficulty finding clear plastic straws, check by telephoning some medical supply companies. You may have to settle for just anything available.) Once the child gets the fluid through a straw, he will be all set to try harder sucking exercises.

Put some Kool-Aid or chocolate milk in a squatty, rather

wide jar that won't tip over easily. A peanut butter jar is fine, but remove the label. Blow a few bubbles in the liquid, then put the straw aside for a minute. Hold the child's hand in front of your mouth and breathe in and out, heavily, a few times. Pucker your lips as if you were holding a straw. Have him do it and feel the air go in and out.

Blow bubbles again. Hold the straw out of the liquid and let him feel the air at the end of it as you breathe in and out, in a very big way. Have him do this, and then let him try sucking with the straw in the liquid. He can see the liquid come up the straw. This first lesson may take more than five minutes. It may take several lessons, but keep trying. Be sure it's all a game and don't give up—this may be very hard and very messy—but keep trying and trying.

When the child succeeds in getting the liquid in his mouth just once, he will be likely to continue sucking through a straw, and you have won quite a victory.

Should this not work satisfactorily, here's another way to try. Put a folded terry kitchen towel under the jar because we're going to spill quite a lot. Fill a wide, squatty jar (peanut butter jar) right to the top with some drink of the child's own choice. (It's a good idea to let the child select what he wants to "drink" through a straw, each lesson. Kool-Aid or any drink that has a definite color.)

Place the short straw in the drink so that just about a quarter of an inch is above the fluid. Put your fingers in the jar to hold the straw. You have already practiced the blowing and breathing in and out. Put the tip of the straw in between the child's lips and say, "Blow!—now drink." His lips are actually in the fluid, and the chances are pretty good he'll get a gulp of it. If he doesn't, try again—after you wipe his mouth and chin and smile some encouragement. If he does get a mouthful, he'll likely want to try again and again. Each time, lift the straw a bit higher above the surface of the liquid. This system has been successful with very severely handicapped children. It's messy but laugh it off—it's worth it. Just clean up the mess and be happy about it.

You may need to resort to using a small, soft plastic squeeze bottle in which you insert a straw. Fill the bottle about two-thirds full of the child's choice of liquid. Place the straw in his mouth, then say, "Blow—now drink," and squeeze the bottle so some liquid will squirt up through the straw. This will take some practice on your part. This works with some cerebral-palsied children who have trouble closing their lips around a straw.

When the child has learned to suck through a straw, use a straw for all fluids for a while. He can get just so much milk with one suck, then he must swallow. As he becomes aware of fluid that is in his mouth because he sucked it in, and swallows it, he should be aware of the presence of saliva and swallow it. Some severely handicapped children have gained control of a protruding tongue, "automatically" swallowing, and of drooling as soon as they have learned to suck through a straw.

Now you can make it a harder and a better exercise by using a longer straw, and thicker fluid such as creamed soups or milkshakes.

The fancy plastic straws with cowboys and clowns make the child really work. It's fun to see the "treat" come up through the loops and twists of the lariat-shaped straw. Be sure you wash these fancy straws with hot water as soon as used. You can't clean them if you allow them to dry out before rinsing. You must rinse them right away. You can find these novelty straws in toy stores, sometimes in supermarkets or souvenir stores. Just keep your eyes open for them. They pop up in the strangest places!

Chewing Exercises

Many handicapped children are fed baby foods or junior foods too long, because they don't like to chew and they rebel. Their fear of choking can become almost panic if they get anything hard or lumpy in their mouths.

You can help them in several ways. Smooth, cooked cereal, such as Cream of Wheat or Ralston, can be served, thinned with milk. Decrease the amount of milk every few days until the cereal is quite thick. Do the same thing with mashed potatoes.

Arrowroot cookies are available in all grocery stores. They are not crumbly, and if a child gets a piece in his mouth, he won't choke. Candy that will melt quickly, yet is crunchy to start with, is good. Don't use anything too sticky at the beginning of these exercises. The child who has not learned to chew will become frightened very easily. *Do not take hold of his jaw to help him if he shows fright.* Direct his attention to your own jaw by pointing to it. Move your jaw in a chewing motion.

Gradually adding thicker foods takes a lot of time, but it is worth while. Well mashed-up baked potatoes with a little finely chopped ground beef is good. The beef can gradually be coarsened. When you have gotten him far enough to accept this he is probably over the stage of being panicky with semisolid food, and you can put your hand under his jaw to help him.

All of these exercises to learn to use the tongue, lips, and jaw must be done at the same time you give the listening lessons. It is likely that your child will learn all these exercises before he has finished the learning-to-listen lessons, which are described in the next chapter.

Be sure your child's teeth are not hurting him. If he has

not been chewing, his teeth may need attention. You can't expect him to chew if it hurts him.

Our developmentally retarded children suffered from lack of dental care for many years, because dentists found it almost impossible to work on them. Not only was the child terrified, but the parents were very uptight and nervous about getting the child to the dentist, and things were disastrous.

This is a specialized field in dentistry, and the larger dental schools have special training for their students, and special clinics just for our special children.

For some children, especially cerebral-palsied children, who are not able to hold their mouth open and jaw steady for even a few seconds, it may be necessary to put the child to sleep so the dentist can do all the necessary work quickly and in one visit. Of course, it takes time to put the child to sleep, to do the work, and attend to the child while he recovers from the anesthetic; but unless the work is very extensive, it is usually all done in one session. It is actually a surgical procedure.

If you think the fee is very high for such an operation, remember that the work done in one visit might have needed as many as ten visits if done without an anesthetic. In addition, special equipment is needed, plus the full attention of a nurse during the entire operation.

You can help your child to accept and to cooperate with the dentist if you prepare him for the visit. Don't talk about it with dread and fear. Talk about what is really going to happen. Tell him the dentist is your friend.

Don't fib. Tell the child it may hurt a little, just like getting a shot, but it won't hurt very long. Play the dentist—act it all out—ham it up—use rewards (at home) as the child learns, from you, to accept the towel under his chin, to put his head back, open his mouth. Poke around, gently, put a tiny bit of water in his mouth and teach him to spit it out, tell him about the "zzz" sound he will hear. Act it all out.

Of course you have taught him to clean his teeth properly, so he knows how to swish water around his mouth and spit it out.

In the kindergarten and primary classes in our special schools, we play doctor and dentist over and over again. The school nurse can be a big help if she has learned about the reward system. (See page 52.)

The dentist trained to work on our special children is usually a very kind and cooperative person. The first visit is usually just a visit to explore the office, to sit in the chair, to feel the towel put on, to lean back, open the mouth, and maybe that's all for an introduction. Preparation at home, at school, and at the dentist's works wonders.

To find dentists who specialize in working with handicapped children, call your local Dental Society. Just look in the telephone book or ask your own dentist how to reach the nearest Dental Society office. It will help the dentist if you have a brief story written for him about your special child so he will know what to expect and what to prepare for. Go to the dentist's office *without* your child to meet the dentist and give him your written story. Then when you arrive for that first visit with your child, you will be greeted as a friend, and that helps your child accept both the dentist and his assistant. They are ready to call the child by his first name and welcome him.

7

Learning to Listen

A CHILD MUST CLIMB many steps before he reaches the goal, that is, using words with meaning, or talking. Just learning to pay attention, to stop and listen, is not very easy and is so very important for all learning. The child must listen and look. A deaf child can't hear so he can't listen. A blind child can't see so he can't look, and it is very hard for these children to learn to pay attention. A child with retarded development may hear and see all right but must learn to use his hearing and seeing. This is what listening and looking is all about—using hearing and seeing properly and profitably and this is called *paying attention.*

It is not possible to teach a child anything unless he first learns to pay attention. A great deal of patience is needed to help the child through this learning-to-listen time. The entire family, including grandparents, must know what you are doing and understand that you need their understanding and cooperation.

The learning-to-listen time does not go fast and smoothly. It takes a long time. Many grown-ups confuse a child with retarded development by expecting him to understand what they are saying before he is able to understand or attach real meaning to the words used.

Mothers naturally talk to their babies while they are holding them. The imitating and talking games that can be so much fun and a delight for children with normal development do not take place between the mother and her child with retarded development because too many words confuse him. Often this child is not *ready* to begin to listen, and this may be misunderstood as not being able or not wanting to listen and learn. The mother or father may even say, "He just *won't* listen."

While holding your child or when sitting close to him, talk to him. Say his name, name his clothing while dressing or helping him to dress, name his food while feeding or helping him to eat. This is called *labeling* and is very important. A parent may have to keep up this labeling for a long time.

Don't get discouraged if your child does not try to talk within a month or a year. Readiness for doing certain things is different in all human beings. We know that children with normal hearing can learn to associate sound symbols (words) with an object, a person, or an action. Some may need much more time to learn what words really mean.

All sounds have meaning and are related to something; a person, object, or action. For example, the opening of the refrigerator door means food is on its way; a telephone rings and someone goes to the phone; a vacuum cleaner noise means mother is cleaning the floor. A child must learn to relate these everyday familiar sounds to what is going on and who is doing it before he can move on to the more difficult step of attaching meaning to words. Just teaching that the telephone's ring or the vacuum cleaner's noise won't hurt you and is a part of everyday life is very important.

Later we will talk about how to help your child learn about noises that will be around him all his life. It's not so bad when a child is afraid of these loud, disturbing noises. Some children who grow up in boarding homes or institutions never hear some of these everyday noises—they never hear sirens or see fire engines. Just try to imagine how terrified you would be if you first heard a fire engine siren and you were ten years old! No wonder our little children cover their ears quickly when a strange sound storms at them.

Many ways can be found to help your child learn the meaning of familiar sounds. If he is afraid of the telephone, turn the ring volume down. When the telephone rings, point to the phone or take him to it. Say "phone" or "telephone" and let him put his ear to the receiver. Give him as many clues as possible about the sound you want him to learn. When you turn on the television, show him what you are doing. The idea is to make him become aware of the sounds around him. Some children will run to listen to certain TV commercials and pay close attention when they don't seem to pay attention to any other sounds or to words from grown-ups. The child needs help to learn about the sounds around him so he must be taught in a very careful way. You must plan how you are going to teach him and plan a time to work with him. Too many noises are confusing and too many words are confusing.

Children with retarded development have trouble sorting out the sounds to find just the kernel of an idea of what the sounds or words mean. So you need a quiet place to work with your child and plans to teach him the meaning of sounds and words beginning with one sound at a time. Just learning where a sound is coming from is a lesson to be learned.

Some children with retarded development find the human voice more interesting than sounds made by things in the house like the telephone or other household noises. You will need to study and watch your child to find out what sounds he pays the most attention to and seems to like the best. Many children are just not ready to pay attention and listen to the things they must learn about. We must start with something very real to him; use the real object, the real thing that he sees or hears every day. Pictures or the TV will be useful later. Things that a child sees or experiences each day will be the words to start with. Here are some words that are good for starters. These words are in daily life and because they are short they are easy to understand or attach meaning to:

ball	baby	cup	book	bath	door
eat	bunny	up	car	down	pot or potty
milk	bird	more	shoe	bed	no
mama	box	yes			

These are the words *most* children learn and use first. Maybe your child may not be associating a word with the object, but he is learning to listen and look at you while you are talking. Some parents say that listening to music has been their child's only response to the world of sound.

In the classroom we start to teach a child to listen and to learn that different sounds mean different things by using noisemakers, such as jingly bells, maracas, and rhythm sticks or drums. For bells you can use a set of bells made for use in rhythm bands, a circle of tape with bells fastened on it, or even an old-fashioned dinner bell. A maraca or dried gourd rattle can be bought at any music store. Rhythm sticks are just two three-quarter-inch dowels, ten inches long. You can buy them at a music store or make them yourself.

Now let's get settled down and start to work. Sit close beside your child at a table. As in earlier lessons, use a low table, comfortable for your child.

Put a jingle bell on the table and then pick it up and shake it. Put it down again. Let him pick it up and shake it. Do this a few times, then put it out of sight.

Next put a maraca or a rattle (not a baby rattle) on the table, then shake it. Let him do it. Let him play with the maraca and the bell, picking them up one at a time and shaking them. Then take them away gently.

Get the child busy with some plastic blocks or a soft toy. Shake the bell or the maraca where he can't see it. When he looks for it, stop, put a "Where is it?" expression on your face and then make the sound again. When he looks for the maraca or even turns his head a little bit, give it to him whether he finds it or not and reward him. (See page 52 for use of rewards.) Stack up the blocks or get his attention back to the table and shake the bells again out of his sight. Do this a few times.

It is important that he enjoy this.

At the next lesson, be sure that you review the entire process again. When he is busy with some toy, then shake the bell out of sight. When he looks for it, show him both the bell and the maraca. He should reach for the one that made the noise. If he does not, offer him the right one and shake it for him. Do this until he can choose the right one. It may take many sessions to learn to do this. Don't be discouraged. Keep trying. And don't forget to reward him.

As he learns the difference between the bell and the maraca, change the maraca for a drumstick or rhythm stick. Go through the same business. *Be sure he knows what is making the noise he hears.* Then change the bell to a squeaky toy and add other things that make noise. Try to find a toy kitty that meows, or a toy cow that moos, or a toy bird that cheeps. (Using a whistle or a horn won't work because he can see you.) Use only two at a time. Trying to choose from three noises is too difficult at this point. This is a fun game, and you should try it every day for a minute or two, even after it is learned.

Learn to play games such as "Open, shut them" (see Songs and Finger Plays in Appendix K).

Put a toy boat and a ball in the bathtub during the child's bath. Pick up the boat and say "boat." Don't say anything else. Do the same thing for the ball. Once is enough the first day. You can say it two or three times the second day. Let him play with them in the tub. Whenever he reaches for one of them say "boat" or "ball." Reward him.

After a few days of this bathtub play, it's time to try these toys on dry land. Place the ball in front of the child on the high-chair tray or table. Say "ball." Do the same thing with the boat. Now place the ball in front of him and say, "Show me ball." Do the same for the boat. You may have to take your child's hand, place it on the ball and say, "Touch the ball." It is just as good to say it this way.

At the next lesson, start the same way as a warm-up. Show him the boat and say "boat." Then show him a ball and say "ball." Repeat the same game saying, "Show me" or "Touch the boat." Then do the same again with the ball. When you are sure he knows what these words mean, you can go on to the next step.

Put the ball away and show him a bell. Ring the bell and say "bell." Put it down. Pick up the boat. Say "boat." Put it down beside the bell.

Say, "Show me bell" or "Touch bell"; then, "Show me boat." Then bring the ball back and have him choose between the ball and the bell. Then the boat and ball, one after another. As he learns to show you the right thing each time, you may add one new thing and take one away, making new combinations of things from the word list. For some children it may be easier to learn names of objects that begin with different beginning sounds. For example, the added clues of using a toy duck and saying the word "duck" may be necessary for the child who just does not seem to understand the game.

Always start a lesson with something you are sure he can do and end the lesson with something you are sure he can do. Your child must feel successful after each lesson, even if you have actually put his hand on the right object for him each time. Suddenly, one day, he will catch on. Time, patience, a smile, and a soft voice are the best tools for success with your child.

Remember that the names of the toys or objects that you use to play this game should have only one or two syllables. For example:

| baby | bunny | box | shoe | milk | door |
| book | bird | car | cup | bed | potty |

These words are easy and common everyday children's words. When you have taught your child to hear these words that have meaning to him, you must try a harder step. Your child is going to select the toy by hearing the word for it without you pointing to the toy.

Until now, you have shown and named each thing first.

Now you are just going to name it and he will show it. You use the same objects and follow the same plan, using two things at a time.

Place two things in front of him, a ball and a cup or book. Now you can say, "Give me ball." Hold out your hand to receive it, and as he gives it to you, say the word "ball" and smile.

Do this for the next lessons until he can give you the right toy every time. Have him find the right one from three toys after he gets pretty good at it. When he can pick out all the toys by name, you can move to the next step.

This a little harder. Put a box about the size of a shoe box or a basket near the child. Use the same toys one at a time at first. Show him the ball. Say "ball." Then say, "Put ball in box," showing him with your hand what to do.

Do the same thing with all the toys until each has been put in the box. Then take all of them out and place two toys in front of him, the bell and the cup. Name one of them— say "bell" without showing him with your hands—then say, "Put bell in box." He is remembering your action as he chooses the right toy.

Do this for a few lessons until he is good at *selecting the right toy and following a direction to do something with the toy.* Be sure you start each lesson with a review, naming each article as you place it in the box.

Now we are ready for the word "listen."

Your child really has been listening, but now he must learn what this word "listen" means. He must learn to look right at you and try hard to understand what you mean.

Put the box on the table and place one toy in front of him. For example, let's use the car.

Say, "Car—put car in box." Guide his hand to be sure he does it right. Say it again, while slowly guiding his hand:

"Car—put car in box." If he moves his hand in the general direction of the car, *reward him.*

Next, place the ball in front of him. Say, "Ball, give me ball." Guide his hand again, toward you this time to be sure he does it right.

Start again and do the same two things, first, "Put car, in box," then, "Give me ball." He must listen to do this.

After doing this two times, put the ball in front of him and say, "Ball—give me ball." If he starts to put it in the box, gently take hold of his hand and say, "No—listen—give me ball." Hold your hand out for it and smile! Do this once again, one time saying, "Put car in box," and the next time saying, "Give me ball." You can mix them up when he begins to learn what you mean. Guide his hand away from making a mistake. He must get the feeling of success.

Don't feel that you are pampering him too much. Praising him for each success will teach him more quickly than scolding or being cross. Sometimes just a tiny lead in the right direction is all he needs, and he will need fewer and fewer leads as he learns to listen and follow the directions.

It may be necessary to capture his attention by gently taking his chin in your left hand and slowly waving your right hand in front of his face, then moving your right hand toward your mouth, then saying, "Listen—give me ball." As you say these words, point to your mouth with your hand but don't cover it. His eyes will follow your hand moving toward your mouth. His eyes must help tell him what to do.

Always be gentle and smiling. Keep changing the objects, selecting from these toys—baby, book, bunny, bird, box, car, shoe, and cup. Smile and reward him.

He is learning to listen carefully.

8

First Words for Comfort and Safety

FOR HIS OWN PROTECTION, every child should learn his own name as soon as it is possible to teach it to him. If your child has a name that is very hard to say, give him a nickname that is easy. You may love his real name, but please call him something *he* can say. This is very important. If he gets lost and is picked up by a policeman, he may not be able to say where he lives or give his full name, but he can identify himself and not be too upset when the policeman says, "Sure, Pat (or Bob, or Mike, or Sue), we'll find your Mommy."

If he is unable to say his name, teach him where his ID name tag is and how to show it to someone, particularly to a policeman. You'll find police officers are very cooperative. Just stop in your local police station and tell the person in charge that you would like to have your child meet a policeman so he won't be afraid if he ever needs to talk to one.

Many police departments have a special service called "Officer Friendly." This is an officer trained and working throughout the schools to acquaint children with policemen. These men are carefully selected and do a very fine job. If you call your local police department, and they don't have such a service, you just might offer the idea to get such a service started.

The ID tag may be worn on a chain around the neck, as a bracelet or a pin (if the child will let it alone). The tag should be engraved with child's name, parents' name, address, and phone number. ID tags and chain range in price from a very nominal sum to more expensive for good stainless steel. (See Appendix F for address to order name tags.)

It is a good idea to sew a fairly good sized patch on the inside of a jacket, with full name, parents' name, address, and phone number. This helps in school, and the child can learn to recognize his own name and address as well as to claim his own jacket.

In addition to his name, there are a few other words your child must learn for his own safety and comfort. You must train him to know these words and to obey them.

These words are "potty," "no," "come to me," "don't touch," "hot," and "sit down." "Okay" is also a helpful word.

Very few children are successfully toilet trained before they can say some word or use a gesture to convey the idea that they want to go to the toilet. The words used by most children all over the world for this idea are natural and easy to say, but society does not accept them, so the child must be taught one acceptable and easy-to-say expression. "Toidy" is hard to say. "Potty" is easier and is quite acceptable.

Parents and all other adults in the family must agree on the same word so as not to confuse the child with a lot of other terms.

Teach your child the word "potty" during the learning-to-listen time and include it in the first words you teach him to say.

"No" is a very important word. You must teach the meaning of "no" just as soon as your child is old enough to begin to do things that are not acceptable, such as grabbing for eyeglasses, throwing food on the floor, biting, or destroying playthings. If you don't want him to do these things, say "no" sternly, and mean it. Shake your finger in his face and say "no," tighten up your stance, look cross, frown sternly for about ten seconds, looking right into his eyes. Hold his chin gently, and wave your finger in front of your eyes to keep him looking at you—then relax, smile, give him a big hug.

Now he might do the same thing right over again. So you repeat the act. If, after three tries, it does not work, you lost that round, so frown again and just turn your back on him and leave him. Try your level best to ignore whatever he does next to get your attention for a few minutes. Then shift to another activity; forget and forgive and better luck next time. It works, so don't give up.

Sometimes a child will laugh when you do this "no" act. Just say "No! Not funny"—and frown harder. "No—not funny" can be a very powerful disciplinary gimmick.

Just plain "no" is the word he must learn. You should say it firmly and then smile as if you are confident that he will mind you. It won't take long until he understands.

If you want your child to understand what he is expected to do, you must train yourself to use only a very few words when talking to him. This is very difficult for parents to do. When they have been asked to try it in the examining room of the clinic, many of them have been surprised to find out how hard it is to limit themselves to the first few necessary words. But unless you do, the child will be confused. It will take time to undo this confusion, but it must be done. A child who has too many words showered on him will stop listening or even trying to learn to listen. *And if he doesn't learn to listen, he can't learn to talk.*

Just saying "no" or "hot" or "sit down" or "don't touch" may sound cross and unkind, but with a little practice it can be done firmly and kindly, in a way that makes the child want to please you.

You should practice this just by yourself in front of a mirror. Look at yourself, say "no," frown, and then smile. You may feel very silly, but if it means your child is happier you can—and you must—do it.

You must not punish your child under any circumstances when he is learning to obey these words.

If he comes to you when you say, "Come to me," you must *smile* and let him know *that* was what you wanted. But don't say, "Come to me," if you want to scold or punish him. *You will never win that way.* What you want is for him to understand and obey your commands, and you must not punish him when he does. If he needs to be punished, go get him yourself and then blow off your steam. Don't make a fool out of him by letting him think he tried to please you and was spanked because he came to you. This same principle is true for all the "must" words.

Both parents should work together to play "come to me." Each should have some little (very little) bits of cookie (or potato chip), something the child likes, in a pocket and Daddy should have a small favorite toy. Don't let him know you have these tidbits when you start. Mother should take him by the hand and walk about fifteen feet away from Daddy, then turn around. Daddy says, "Come to me," holding a favorite toy in his hand. He should squat down on his heels with his arms stretched out, he should smile and say it very gently.

When the child comes to you, love him, give him the toy and a piece of cookie. If he does not move toward Daddy, Daddy must keep saying gently, "Come to me," and keep smiling. Mother should walk slowly, slightly ahead of the child, holding one hand, pulling him gently and pointing to Daddy with the other hand. When he gets close to Daddy, give him the cookie and a big hug anyway. Try it again. Make it a game. Don't chatter. Mother can say "cookie" or "Daddy" if she can't keep quiet. You can always say "good boy" or "good girl," or "big boy" or "big girl." Play the game many times and play it often until your child can play it easily.

You can teach "sit down" in a little game. Line up two dining room chairs and a little chair for the child. Daddy slaps the chair seat, says "Sit down," and sits down; Mother does the same thing. The chances are the child will sit when you turn to him, slap the chair seat, and say, "Sit down." Make your child enjoy it and he will learn this necessary command. You may have to slap the chair each time for a while, but *always smile when you do it.* Be sure to let him know he did the right thing. Reward him.

You may have to bend him gently in the middle the first few times. If you have to do this, smile, and say, "Sit down" as you bend him. *Never pick him up and slam him in the chair.*

"Don't touch" is very important. The first step is to let him touch a few things under your direction. He will be satisfied with this and won't want to touch so many taboo things.

A new lamp is usually a very beautiful thing to a child. Take him to it, say, "Pretty" as he reaches for it, guide his hand to feel its lovely base and pretty shade, say, "Pretty." Then, holding his hands gently and shaking your head, say, "Don't touch, break." *Do not sound cross.* It's the fast pass or grab at something a child longs to touch that causes trouble. Satisfy his curiosity and he won't grab so much.

Show him the things he must not touch. For the sake of any handicapped child, don't have too many things around that are taboo. Let him touch your new earrings or new perfume bottle, then let him know he must not touch.

Eyeglasses cause trouble with children with retarded development. Get your child a pair of inexpensive plastic glasses to play with, and he will be satisfied to let others alone.

Give him a purse of his own. Put a few things in it. Then he can be told not to touch Mother's purse. Give him some keys of his own and a comb. Let him know he can have them. Use his own name to teach this. Show him your purse and say, "Don't touch"; then show him his purse, say "Tommy's," pushing it gently toward him.

The flowers in the garden, especially the neighbor's garden, stir up a lot of trouble. If you let your child feel and smell a flower or two, actually put one in his hand while you say, "Pretty" and "M-m-m-good" as you smell it, he won't be so anxious to grab them. After he has had a good look, teach him to look at them and smell them, but "don't touch."

Try to get your neighbor to help you. Explain that your child is handicapped or developmentally disabled or delayed and is not as quick as other children to understand that flowers are to be enjoyed, not pulled up by the roots. Show your own understanding of what your neighbor's garden means to her and let her know that you want your child to learn to enjoy her flowers. Ask her to do with him as you have done—let him hold a flower in his hand, say "Pretty," and then, gently, "Don't touch," and smile at him. Ask her to show him around the garden and, if it is a showplace, point out to her diplomatically that "good fences make good neighbors," and fence in your own yard if possible.

This training to obey certain words begins as soon as you have started your program with your child. It is just as important as the lip and tongue exercises.

Remember that now the lessons are aimed at three things:

1 Lip and tongue exercises
2 Learning to listen
3 Learning to obey certain key words

Your lessons are busy times and must be pleasant times, too. And now it's time to say words.

9

Saying Real Words That Mean Something

A CHILD USUALLY WILL SAY a word that means something only after he has learned to listen to enough sounds and word-sounds that have real meaning to him.

Sometimes you will be surprised to hear a child say some well-spoken words before you think he is ready to try them. These "surprise" words could be almost anything and far more difficult than you would expect to hear first. Children who say words beyond your expectations may stop talking after that surprise speech and then follow the usual learning pattern. Or they may go on saying words and following no set pattern for what should come next. But don't count on a handicapped child's speaking "surprise" words; it seldom happens.

When you feel quite sure that the child is well acquainted with the word-sounds through the listening lessons, it is time to start to say the words for the now-familiar objects. The first words are the same ones that we used to identify and then to name the objects for listening lessons. They begin with *b*, *p*, and *m*.

We use these words because we must start with sounds

your child can see and feel as well as hear. Watch yourself in a mirror and say "boat." Notice how your lips move. Put your hand in front of your lips and feel the air pop out when you say "boat." Put your hands on your voice box (Adam's apple) and feel the vibration.

Now, still in front of the mirror, say "car" or "gun." You won't see any movement nor will you feel any air pop out.

To give a handicapped child as much help as possible to say a word-sound, you let him use his senses of hearing, seeing, and feeling.

Step One

Let's take our favorite ball for an example.

Show the ball to the child; say "ball."

Hand it to him, cupping it in both his hands, and say "ball" again.

Direct his eyes to your mouth as you say "ball" (exaggerate it!).

Take the ball in one of your hands, holding it right in front of you; take the child's hand and hold it to your lips as you say again "ball." He can feel your lips pop open and the air escape as you say it.

Quickly and gently move his hand to his own lips and say, "Say ball."

He will very likely give you a "ba—" sound and that will be wonderful. Reward him.

If his lips move the least bit toward forming a *b* rejoice because you are really getting somewhere. You say "ball" for him and give him a big hug.

Keep trying a few times. If you cannot get him to give you more than the *b* sound, put his hand on your Adam's apple as you say "ball," then move his hand to his own Adam's apple. He can feel the vibration of the "aw" sound in his voice box.

If your child has learned his listening lessons well, he should produce a "ba—" sound with a few tries.

Go on to the other favorite words from the *b* list, using first the objects he learned to select most easily. These objects are old friends and will be easier for him to name.

Each time let the child *hear the name of the object, see* the object, *see* you say it, *feel* the object, *feel* you say it, and *feel* himself say it. Work with these favorite words until he can say them quite well with the help of hearing, seeing, and feeling. Finishing Step One might take a few weeks.

Step Two

Now you must move on to saying the word without letting him feel the object or your lips; he will only *see* it and *hear* it named.

Use "bus" this time.

Show it to him. Say, "Bus—say bus." He may need to hold it in his hand and look at your lips as you repeat it, but he should be able to say it without touching your lips. Get him to "graduate" from needing to hold the object as soon as possible.

Work on this step until he can name a lot of objects. It is true that these first words are parrotlike. Your child is just saying what you say, imitating you. He must go through this to get used to hearing himself make meaningful sounds. When he starts to give you words by just seeing the object or picture of an object, he is *saying* words, and he is on the way to *using* words.

Step Three

Now the child can say the names of these favorite objects when he *sees* the object only; he no longer needs to hear its name or feel it. You select an object and show it to him without saying anything. He must depend upon his own "memory of things heard" to say the right word.

This is a big step forward, and your child is almost ready to *use* words, instead of just *saying* words. His eyes help him to remember the sound of what you want him to say.

Step Four

Now the child must say the word on his own and not take his pattern directly from you. Let him select an object and name it without your *telling* him or *showing* him.

The word he says is now his own to use without your help.

Of course, these are only a few words, the names of some familiar toys. This taste of success opens the door to more effort and confidence in trying to "talk."

A word of warning—do not skip any of these steps. Your child needs practice at each step to gain confidence to try new words later on.

You will use the same objects you used for learning to listen: ball, boat, bell, baby, etc. (the *b* list on page 205).

As these words come easily, you can add to these objects and mix them in with the familiar objects already learned.

box	bottle
pipe	bed (dollhouse)
pan	beads
book	bath (dollhouse)

bird   potty (dollhouse)
bunny   buttons (on a string)

Keep your box of objects out of sight and take out only five or six for each lesson. Keep changing every day, but be very sure you always have *two* favorite toys that your child can name easily so he can be sure of some success.

When most of these objects can be named easily, it is time to start to use pictures instead of objects. Follow the directions in the back of this book to get your pictures ready.

It will take a little time to shift from naming a real ball to naming a ball in a flat picture. Try to get a picture of a ball as nearly as possible like the ball you have been using.

Some children have a hard time learning that a picture of something is the same thing as the real thing. For example, when a child has learned to identify and maybe to label many common objects such as a ball, a bottle, a potty, he may not recognize a picture of a ball as the same thing. The picture is flat and cannot be picked up. This does not happen very often but when it is a problem, here are two ways to help to learn the meaning of pictures. First, as in all teaching, the child's attention must be captured.

1. Flocking or some other rough surface may be pasted or sprayed on the picture so the child can feel the picture. Many Christmas cards and greeting cards are flocked. These are great, especially if it is a picture of Santa Claus with his beard and fur trimmings flocked so when touched, the rough surface gains the child's attention. You buy velour paper in hobby shops or from school supply companies. Cut out small bits and paste them on parts of the picture. Stroke the picture and help the child do the same thing as you say the word that names the picture.

2. Another way to attract attention to a picture is to use a

Polaroid camera. Stand beside the child in front of a long mirror. Point to the child in the mirror, touch him, touch him in the mirror, saying his name with each movement. Now without any time delay take a picture of the child, have him watch you pull the picture out of the camera, and hold it beside him in front of the mirror so he can see the picture and himself. Be sure to say his name each time he sees himself, when you touch him, when you look at the picture and again when you point to his reflection in the mirror. Reward him when he looks at his own picture and when he looks at himself in the mirror. Repeat this game, taking pictures of members of the family, pets, and favorite toys or treasures. You will not need to do this many times before he gets the idea that a picture can be something real.

When you must resort to the Polaroid camera technique, pictures on cards or in books hold very little meaning. The child must first make the connection between real people, and real things that have meaning to him, and the pictures of those people and things.

When you show pictures, do not lay them flat on a table. Children with Downs Syndrome have a particularly difficult time looking at anything flat on a table. Use a small easel to hold them at about a 30-degree angle from the tabletop. You want the kind that folds back on itself, the cover fastening into the back in such a way that a photograph will stand up by itself. Lay this easel on its back and you have the correct angle to hold pictures. This is like the angle on the lectern in church. You will use these easels, as you will use your box of objects, for many lessons later on. You will come back to them again and again. (You can make one yourself following directions in Appendix C, or obtain one from a local photographer.)

Start with a picture of a ball and a picture of a baby. Keep these face down on the table. Have the real ball and the baby doll on the table.

Place the picture of the baby on the easel and say, "Baby —baby—show me baby." If he *points to the picture*, say, "Good," "baby" and pick up the baby doll. If he *picks up the baby doll* first say, "Good," "baby" and hold the doll beside the picture and say "baby." Reward him.

Now change pictures; place the picture of the ball on the easel. Do the same thing with the ball and the picture of the ball that you did with the doll and the picture of the baby.

Say, "Ball—ball—show me ball," and so on.

Continue doing this, using only two things at a time for a few days. You may feel this is too easy and be tempted to rush ahead. Don't do it. You must be sure the child knows that he should say the same word for both picture and object.

When you feel sure he can select the baby, ball, bus, bell, and boat by seeing the pictures, you can try a harder step.

Now you will need the pocket chart (see page 215).

Place three easy pictures on the chart: for example, the bell, box, and bunny. Place a real box in front of the child. Don't say the word, just say, "Find it," moving your hand in the general direction of the picture of the box. If he has trouble, you may say "box" and hold the box up to the picture. Help him a little because you must not let him fail at first. You want him to learn that the picture and object are the same thing. He will find it by himself with less and less help.

As he shows you the correct picture, say the word and ask, "What is this?" He should say the correct name. Reward him.

You might have to help him just a little bit by directing his attention to your lips, set to say the word. Sometimes it helps to touch the child's upper lip to remind him to pull it down a bit to get a *b* sound.

Later when he selects the right picture you can just say, "What is this?" without saying it for him first. When you have reached this stage, you are really ready to move on into using words, lesson planning will be easier, and you can feel that you have led your child a long way toward communicating with his world.

10

Learning about What Is "Different" and What Is "Alike"

As a child grows in his ability to attach meaning to words and is being taught to use more and more words, he learns very easily that things are not all alike. If the child did not learn that sounds are different, and words are different, he would not bother to use words. He would not need to. Just as a baby learns to cry in different ways to let you know how things are, he learns to make sounds, and then to use words to tell you, "I mean this and not that."

In working with your child start to use the word "different" before you use the word "alike." Children can notice differences before they notice that some things are alike. This order of development, noticing differences before noticing likenesses, is a normal growth pattern.

Even the caveman hunter, returning to his cave from a long hunt, must have noticed immediately if something were different from what it was when he left for his safari. But, if everything were just the same, he would likely have no comment.

So it is with children learning about likeness and differences. In planning lessons, make up tasks that demand that differences be noticed. Later the demand will be to notice what things are alike.

Learning about differences is actually learning to discriminate. Judgments must be made to discriminate. In learning to listen, a child learns to discriminate, to make judgments that this sound means this, and that sound means something different. As judgments are made the child can make practical use of the information he gets and can put things together either to form meaningful and more complex ideas, or to do more difficult tasks such as gathering all the things needed for a chore, or for assembly work.

As the child learns to use his eyes and hands, as well as his ears, to discriminate, he needs many opportunities to experience differences.

We learn to discriminate by size, shape, color, and feel, in this order. Some children learn about color early because mothers tend to name colors while dressing a child. In planning a teaching program, you should follow this order and start with size first.

The child must see something big and touch and explore its bigness, then see something little and touch and explore its littleness.

You start with things around you all the time: a big chair, a little chair; a big person, a little person; and move on to a big book, a little book; a big bottle, a little bottle; a big cookie, a little cookie. Use a whole collection of familiar things to practice a variety of judgments.

The Multi-Sensory Cubes and Spheres #6255, available from Ideal School Supply Co. (see Appendix G), provides materials for teaching about size, shape, color, and texture. The set is not inexpensive, but you will use it a great deal, and it's well worth the investment. The set contains big and little cubes, big and little balls (spheres), two each in red, blue, and yellow, one of each pair is smooth and the other rough-textured.

You can make up a set of pictures that show a big bottle and a little bottle; a big bar of soap and a little bar of soap; a big jar of peanut butter and a little jar of peanut butter.

When you start to teach "big" and "little," use your voice and be dramatic. When you say "big," use a big deep voice and act giantlike. When you say "little," say it "lit-tle," using a soft tinylike voice. Your child is likely to imitate you.

You can play a game. Stand facing each other. Squat down on your heels, hug your knees, sort of curl up in a little ball and say, in a small voice, "Now, I'm lit-tle."

Jump up straight and stretch high, saying in a great, big voice, "Now, I'm big!" Then say, "You do it"—and as you repeat the performance, help the child imitate you.

(Avoid saying "small" and "tall" for a while. These words sound too much alike for beginners. The nursery song "I'm Very, Very Small" is good for later on when the child knows more words and can listen very carefully.)

Do not use anything to teach "big" and "little" at this time except things that have real meaning and are not strange to the child. After using the full-sized things in the room, use balls, bottles, boxes, bean bags, toy cars.

Another step in learning about size is to put things in the right *order*. This is a good time to use the post and rings to learn to stack by size (see page 218, Ideal School Supply).

Then you line up various-sized blocks according to size, from big to little, or from little to big. You can start to use the words "first" and "last" now. "We put the *big* one *first*; now the next one," etc., and finish with, "the *little* one is *last*." The whole idea of putting things in *order* is very important in the entire learning process. Learning about *first, next,* and *last* is enough for now.

Every child must learn that somehow, someway, *first* things come first, then something follows next, and so on until the *last* thing is the end of a chore.

Be very careful about the words *you* use. Do not try to teach young developmentally retarded children using the comparative forms such as "bigger" or "smaller." This sort of comparison is very confusing. Say, "big one—now the next big one, etc." Socrates discovered this two thousand years ago!

Now let's teach about shapes. Use blocks and balls to start out. If you have the Multi-Sensory Cubes and Spheres mentioned on page 93, use these. If you do not have this material you can make your own sets. Don't use the words "cubes" and "spheres." Call them "blocks" (or "squares") and "balls." It's much easier to understand. You can make square and round bean bags. Use plain cloth, not fancy printed material. Don't stuff them too full! Make six bean bags of each shape, two square red, two square blue, two square yellow, and two round red, two round blue, and two round yellow. You will find many uses for these bean bags.

Caution: Keep these materials for teaching only; put them away with all your teaching supplies so the child won't lose interest by having them to play with all the time. These objects are important for learning about differences and likenesses and must be interesting and fresh for each lesson.

Start with a blue square or block and a blue circle or block. Place the blue square in front of the child and say "square." Then place the blue circle beside it and say "circle." "Show me the circle,"—guide his hand if he does not start to reach for the circle. Repeat, "The circle—show me the circle."

Remember you can say, "Show me," "Put your hand on,"

or "Put your finger on"—whichever direction you have found works best. It is a good idea to stay with the same words. If your child responds better to "Put your hand on —" then use that all the time until he can follow directions successfully; then you can use and mix in the other directions.

As the child learns to identify the square and the circle, either with the bean bags or the blocks, you can use squares and circles cut out of wood or masonite and painted. These are flatter and help the child to move toward recognizing shapes on a flat surface. (See page 218 for DLM material —you can buy these cut-out shapes.)

Next use squares and circles cut out of black construction paper and mounted on white paper. The paper should be about 9″ x 12″ and the squares and circles about 6″ in diameter.

When the child can identify the square and circle easily, you can start to teach the word "round." Say, "The circle is round," and let him trace the edge of the circle with his fingers. Say, "Round, the circle is round" each time he handles it. Then do the same thing with the square, saying, "Square—the square is not round, feel the corners, squares have corners—now feel the circle, circle—round things do not have corners." Find round things in the room, a plate, a tabletop, etc.

Now you can begin to use colors. Teaching colors can be done along with daily speech lessons as your child learns to say words. Use the big red ball, the little yellow ball, a big red toy bus, and a little yellow toy bus. You can combine size, shape, and color with these materials. You can use the bean bags also.

Place the red and the yellow balls in front of the child so he can easily see them both at the same time. Pick up the yellow one and say, "Ball—yellow ball." Put it down again. Do the same thing with the red ball, then say, "Show me the *red ball.*" When he does it, say, "What is it?" If the answer is "ball," you smile, nod your head to mean he is correct, and say, "Ball—a red ball." Pick up the red ball and say, "This is a *red ball.*" Put it down again and say, "Give me the *red ball.*" Reward him.

Go on with this, using either balls or buses until these words are learned. If your child is a "pitcher" and would rather roll or throw the balls, use the bean bags, saying "bean bag" instead of "ball."

You will probably get "wed" for "red," "e-woe" or "e-doe," maybe "we-woe" for yellow, but don't worry about it. If it sounds anything like the right word, it's a good start.

Now we can move along to learning to sort colors. Place a sheet of red and a sheet of yellow construction paper in front of the child. Then put six red and six yellow blocks in a box and keep this in your lap. (These blocks are the 1-inch blocks. See page 218, Milton Bradley or DLM.)

Show the child a yellow block and say "yellow." Place it on the yellow paper. Do the same thing again.

Now show him a red block. Say "red" and place it on the red paper.

Continue this, presenting whatever block you happen to pick up next in the box. You only have two colors in the box this time.

Don't urge him to say the names of the colors. What we want here is matching the block and paper by color.

Another time use green and yellow or red and blue.

Later you can use three colors instead of two, and when he gets good at it, you can sort four colors.

Go slowly and don't be discouraged. All these color words are hard to say. If your handicapped child learns to say red, yellow, blue, and green, he is talking *usefully*—he is doing very well.

Now you can go back a bit and use more ways to teach about size, more ways to teach about shapes. You can add triangle, diamond, and star shapes. You can mix all three discriminating ideas—a big yellow ball, a little blue bus, and so on.

A harder chore is to select all the balls, or blocks, or triangles, regardless of color, from a box of assorted shapes mixed together. From this the child learns that a circle, a triangle, or any set shape is always the same shape regardless of its color or size.

Again you can ask him to find another circle, something round in the room. Help him. This is not easy at first.

Do the same thing with color. Tell the child to find all the things in the box that are *red*—then find other red things in the room, or red in the clothes he or you may be wearing.

You might have better luck just putting the assortment of things in front of him on the table rather than in a box. The top of a shoe box makes a good container. It's not too deep, and things are easily seen—and the little balls can't roll away.

The games we have just talked about depend upon *listening* and *seeing*.

It is a good time to review and to add some more experiences to seeing differences. For example, put two spoons and a key before the child; name each item as you place it; point to each and again name each one; then say, "Which one is different?" or "Show me which one is different." You can make up a lot of sets of common objects to teach this skill. You can use the sets of cut-out squares, circles, and triangles, cut-out squares of different colored construction paper, all kinds of common objects, cups, drinking glasses, keys, crayons, small boxes, empty pill bottles, just about anything you can collect—just be sure the child is familiar with what you use.

Now we can move on to another step, learning about how things feel, texture, as well as size and shape. The child should have some idea by now that some things *feel* big and some things feel little, some feel like squares or blocks because of the corners, some feel round and don't have any corners. Always be sure to let your child handle the things you are using to teach size and shape so his hands help him remember the differences he feels.

It is necessary to learn that things are smooth or rough, soft or hard, wet or dry, sticky or not sticky—that things are different not just because they look different, but because they feel different.

The skills to recognize differences or likenesses can be strengthened by adding games that require the child to feel *differences*.

Use a cloth bag. Put two spoons and a key in the bag. Let the child *see* you put each item in and *hear* you name it. Better still, let *him* put the things in the bag, naming each item after you say it if he can say the words. Then have him reach in the bag and, without looking, find the one that is different. Use the same sets of materials you used for size and shape, adding many sets of objects very familiar to the child, spoons, keys, crayons; just be very sure the things are very familiar and very real. A toy fire truck or a little metal Indian or cowboy is not very real.

When he can find the one that is different each time, then and only then can you move along to finding the two things that are alike. You did a little of this learning about likenesses while working with shape and color, but we did not use the words, *"Find one like this."*

These games to find likenesses are matching tasks.

Place two things on the table, a spoon and a key, old familiar friends, name each one as you put it down. Now show the child another spoon, just like the one on the table, and say, "Spoon, show me another spoon *just like* this spoon." Help him make the match and be sure to reward him. Then repeat, "This spoon is *just like* this spoon." You might even add, "Now we have *two* spoons. They are alike." If this last step seems to confuse the child, wait a while to start to use the number two.

Continue this matching game, using the objects you have collected. Do not use too many during one lesson. It is much better to be sure he can match and see the likenesses in as few as three sets of items than to be guessing a bit too much by having too many decisions and judgments to make.

Now you can use the cloth bag again.

Start out by putting just two things in the bag—one spoon and one key. Now show him another spoon and ask him to find one like it in the bag. Always name the article he succeeds in finding.

The next step would be to put two spoons and one key in the bag and ask him to find two things that are alike. Remember to always name the things he succeeds in finding in the bag.

You can make this task harder and harder by using things that are almost alike, like quarters and nickels, then dimes and pennies, or two kinds of keys, or two sizes of small pill bottles.

As these words that tell about what is different and what is alike become useful, putting words together and using longer sentences helps get ideas across.

Review, reward, and make it all a game.

Learning to search for things that are alike is a big step

forward in learning to associate words, things, people, and their ideas.

Sometimes it seems that the world is arrested in growing up, when people are so hung up on why we are different rather than growing up to try to find out more ways that people are alike. Surely it is easy to recognize that we are all different in appearance and ability. Yet being able to see how human beings are alike with the same deep wishes for comfort and peace and love is truly growing up and maturing.

11

Using Words and Making Sentences

Now we are almost ready to *use* words, not just *say* them.

Before starting to teach a handicapped child to use words and make sentences, it will help you to know how children without the handicap of delayed language develop this skill. When you understand how things would go along normally, you can begin to see how your child is delayed— that is, what steps he is not going through day by day.

You might expect a handicapped child to follow the same developmental patterns the normal child goes through only to move more slowly. This is not so. Handicapped children usually have complications that delay and confuse their ability to develop the skills in a normal flow of development. And because their patterns of development are usually confused, we must not expect one method of teaching to be the answer to "How do I teach a child to build sentences?"

It is necessary to know many ways and to use the way that fits each individual child. It is good to try to use a normal sequence pattern if it works; but as you go along following an expected sequence and find it is not successful, you must try another way.

Another way could be the system used for children with

impaired hearing or some of the gimmicks used to help the visually impaired child. Both of these types of handicapped children have special problems in learning to put words together to form sentences.

So let's review a bit about normal development, learn how most children build sentences, and note some of the things that a handicapped child might find difficult.

When a child starts to *say* words, he may not actually be *using* the words. A word is being *used* when the child says the word to get what he wants or tell you something. A child first says words one at a time, and he will *use* words one at a time. Only when the child is using words to get what he wants across to you, can we expect him to put two or more words together to make sentences, a very difficult task.

When your child begins to label or name the persons, places, and things around him, this is a very exciting time for parents, but especially for parents of a special child. All of the waiting, loving, caring, and teaching has helped the child develop a way to have some of his needs and desires met—a very important step toward independence.

The use of one word can mean many things. When your child says "milk" this means, to his family, "I want a glass of milk" or "I want more milk." It could even direct attention to some spilled milk. Even though the words may not be perfectly said, parents learn to "understand" what he is saying and what he wants.

It is very important that your child learns many words. The lists in Appendix B contain words that have been found to be (1) most often used by preschool children and (2) words that can be pictured.

Notice that the words are grouped in families or categories such as foods, clothing, action, time, color, etc. Children seem to learn the names of things they are doing, seeing, and manipulating. The words are listed alphabetically in each category so you can find them easily, not in order of development or difficulty.

It is helpful to the child to learn groups of words together so that the words can be compared with one another: "That is a hat," "That is a coat," "That is not a hat"; or, "I eat cookies," "I don't eat dirt." Language learning is a very difficult task, and a child with retarded language development needs all the help he can get. Teaching groups of words that go together helps the child to learn new words, to build vocabulary, and to find out about what goes with what.

Any language or speech learning is not just a continued growth of single words, however. Studies of children who are developing speech show that not only does a child continue to increase the number of spoken words he uses, but he also begins to put two words together or in combination without having hundreds of single words. For example, early two-word combinations include:

"see bus"   "daddy car"   "up there"   "more cookie"

The miracle of language becomes more mystifying since children who learn language automatically pick out the important part of the message or those words which convey the meaning of what they are saying. A child does not always use words such as "and," "the," or "a" first. Children can begin to put two words together when they have a vocabularly of just twenty words, and these words can communicate many different things and be used in many different ways:

"more cookie"	"more milk"	"wanna cookie"
"Mommy milk"	"Mommy cookie"	"Mommy bye-bye"
"Daddy up"	"Daddy car"	"eat cookie"

The model or the teacher of a child learning to perform this magic of putting words together is usually his parent. As the teacher or parent, you will likely be talking to the child quite naturally, yet shortening your sentences. If you use a sentence you expect a child to imitate during a lesson or at any other time, the child will not imitate your model completely. You might say, "Here's a cookie," and the child will say only "a cookie" or just "cookie." If you say, "There's a big plane up there," the reply would likely be "big plane there," or "plane there," or maybe just "plane." Children will pick out the important words to imitate and those words are nouns, verbs, and adjectives (see page 232). Whether he actually picks out these words to imitate or does not hear and remember the other helper words is not known for sure. Children will slowly start to put in the helper words themselves as they grow older.

In teaching your child you should use very simple, direct sentences. Some children seem to need to have the model you want imitated cut down as you would with a telegram. Some question exists about the teacher talking like a telegram or using a regular sentence for a model. Try both ways. If your child imitates your model, "See the baby," using all three words, that's fine. If the imitation is just "See baby," and he has dropped "the," try a few more times; if the little words are always dropped then you will likely help him more by using the telegram-type, simpler sentence for imitation. Here are some sample sentences to show how this would be:

"There's a truck"
"See the baby" or "See baby"
"Open"
"Come to me" or "Come here"

The child with retarded language development needs to

have this same kind of short sentence or model used over and over again once he is using single words. He needs this help to go on to putting two words together. This may be difficult for parents whose child may be six years old and is still at the single-word level. But for the child who is developmentally retarded, it is very important to continue to have someone help him go from that one word to putting two words together before we can expect him to speak in complete sentences.

Rules for putting words together are quite clear when a child is progressing normally. The word *handicapped* means that something or some condition is blocking the way for normal progress. So it is with our children whose language development is delayed. They just might go along according to the rules, but many of them do not. We try to follow the recognized rules and happily are surprised that things are going along. So many handicapped children are not able to follow the rules, so we must find other ways for them to learn to put words together. No one set system is the answer for children with handicaps, so we will tell you about several ways that have worked well to produce connected speech, phrases, or sentences.

We start with a system following the developmental rules and then try another way if progress is not being made. Again, remember to shift and change your pace before frustration upsets things. It's hard to know when to try a little bit harder and a little bit longer. If you have been guiding (structuring success) and praising and making lesson time a happy time, you will pick up signals of frustration easily. The signals are unhappiness during a lesson that has been happy and pleasant up to this point.

A word of warning here: don't confuse real frustration with disappointment. If the lesson time keeps your child from some activity he feels he is missing or being left out of, you must set another lesson time to which he can look forward comfortably.

It helps to remember also that lesson time might be the only time your child has you all to himself and that is very precious in a busy family. Don't disappoint him—keep your "date" with him and always try to make it fun and reward him for his successful tries.

When a child starts to ask for "milk" he should hear the needed words "want milk" or "I want milk" or "more milk" from the person that he is asking for the milk. This *does not* mean that you do not give him the milk until he repeats "I want milk," but it does mean that you set the example, you give him the language pattern that he can listen to, as you encourage him to imitate what you are saying. *Encouragement* to imitate is emphasized rather than forcing or making him say "I want milk" before he can have it. It is our belief that when a child is ready to imitate he will imitate the two-word combinations *if* he hears the appropriate model.

Using words should be emphasized again—you say the two or three words together every time he says just "milk." Say it pleasantly, with a smile on your face that means "How about saying it my way?" You may need to keep this up for a long time. When the child does imitate your words and says "more milk" or "I want milk," it does not necessarily mean that he has really learned to use a meaningful sentence. At first, it means that he listened to you, heard what you said, and understood what you said. Very likely he is echoing back to you, imitating you, and quite possibly has used very little of his thinking to say the words at this point. Do not forget to reward him for his success, and success can mean even a very small, but noticeable move toward using words.

When the child actually asks for something or tells you about something, *using* two or more words, his own thinking is guiding him, and he no longer is just imitating. He likely will need to go through the imitating steps again when new and more difficult ideas are coming into his experience.

A word of caution: you must not expect the new learner to have the speech sounds perfect in each word. If he says "wa— mi—" instead of "want milk," repeat his response naturally, "want milk" or "I want milk," rather than calling attention to his error. By providing the model again you can give him an immediate "replay" for comparing his own message.

If the child seems puzzled that you did not say it the way he did, or refuses to try it again, stop, get a drink of water, walk around a bit, then try again; but do it a little differently.

Again give him the good example "want milk"; but if he still says "wa— mi—," repeat it as he said it—smile—let him know you understand and accept his way. If you show displeasure with his imperfect sounds, you could turn him off. Say the words his way for a little while, then when he knows you accept his message, say "wan*t*" stressing the *t* very hard. Just go after the one clipped sound at first. "Milk" is a hard word to say, and the chances are when he gets the idea to put the *t* sound on the end of "want," he will then try to pick up the end sound of "milk."

By setting a good example yourself, you encourage the child to imitate you. Imitating the teacher follows a set pattern. Draw the child's attention to your mouth, either directly or with you both sitting before a mirror. The child needs to see as well as hear what he is expected to imitate. A hug will be reassuring that he is on the right track. At the same time say, "Good talking!"

Some things to remember at this point:
You are the teacher—the language model. You must:

1 *Know how many words* your child can put together by imitation. This gives you some idea of his auditory memory or his memory for spoken words. If you give him a model that is too long, he will cut it back—reduce it—to the length he can remember. Very young children usually will reduce a model sentence to two to four words no matter how carefully you say the model.

2 *Learn to use the most important words* in the idea being conveyed. These words will likely be nouns, verbs, and adjectives, in that order of importance to the child. If necessary, you must reduce your model as you would write a telegram. Since you are trying to limit the number of unnecessary words in a telegram you cut out less important words such as "the," "and," "a," and try to be brief and to the point. Instead of saying "Let's put on your coat and go outside," you can say while putting on his coat, "Coat on." When you are ready to go outside say, "Go out" or "Go outside." This is particularly important to do with the language-retarded child. Just because you are being very brief does not mean you must sound cross or gruff; smile, use a gesture, and keep smiling.

3 *Know that difficulty is due* to the kinds of words used as well as the way the words are put together. The sentence "Is it ten o'clock?" is much harder to say and understand than "I want more cookie." Wanting a cookie is a very real thing to a child. We call such words *concrete*. The words are very definite. You can have a picture to match the word. Words that must be explained—that you cannot use a picture to explain—are called *abstract*. A little child cannot manage abstract words or abstract ideas. He uses only *concrete* words until he is able to understand abstract ideas.

4 *Remind yourself* that repeating words and phrases after you is only a step toward "talking." If your child does not

answer a question, label, or put words together without a cue, then it is important to keep going over things you have seemingly taught him before. You must continue to review. If he does not repeat "it's a ball" when you show him a ball, he should not be expected to answer your question "What is this?" although you know that he knows what a ball is and very likely has said "ball" many times. It is time for you to go back to naming objects rather than just having him imitate or "parrot talk" what you say.

Talking, actually using words, occurs when a child can put words together by himself without imitating someone else to express his own thoughts. Only after a child learns to combine words all by himself is he able to begin experimenting with phrases. A phrase is a meaningful combination of words.

The many stages of speech and language development a young child goes through just seem to happen so easily you hardly notice how very fast the patterns are changing and becoming more complicated. The child with retarded language development, on the other hand, must work very hard to be able to communicate. It is a long way from the beginning of learning to pay attention to learn to listen, to say words, to use words, and then to put words together to communicate ideas.

Again we look at the reports of children developing language skills, and we see that there are similar patterns which happen just as with two-word combinations.

As the child begins to put more words together, or "chain words," he begins to use articles ("the," "an"), pronouns, negatives ("no," "not"), prepositions, and some verbs (see page 232):

Me drink milk.

Milk up there.
That my cookie.
It not my cup.
John a good boy.

Although the putting together of words into phrases sounds strange, children do try out many ways before they get to the most difficult of all, using a complete sentence. If one listens carefully, there is little doubt about what the child is trying to say when he is using phrases. Words are left out but the meaning is there. It is true, each word may not be perfectly said; but the important part of the message is there.

When a child finally speaks in sentences, he has learned not only to put certain words together, but he shows he has picked up and begun to use some basic rules of grammar. Researchers are far from agreeing just how children do this. All we know for certain is that a pattern exists in our language, we can list a set of rules, but exactly how a child learns to follow the rules is still a mystery. Maybe that is why the development of language is sometimes called "magical." It could also be the reason it is so very hard to teach a child to use the rules for good grammar when he does not do it naturally. When we use the word "rules," we mean the patterns that have been observed in normal language development. We do not mean a *rule* or *law* that we actually teach and that must not be broken or violated.

As we said earlier, the use of spoken language or speech to communicate with others does not just happen in a haphazard or hit-and-miss way. Nouns, verbs, and adjectives are used first, then a child learns to use other parts of speech including pronouns, prepositions, conjunctions, and adverbs. People who have made a lifetime work out of studying how children learn to speak use a special set of words to talk about the language process: for example, syntax and transformational grammar. This can be very confusing because the research people do not always agree on the meaning of these terms. (We think that parents will understand when we use terms for the parts of speech and parts of sentences that we all learned about in English classes.)

What is a sentence? "Johnny uptown, Mommy" is not a sentence, but if one fills in the missing words, "Johnny *is* uptown *with* Mommy," we do have a complete sentence. In moving from using phrases to sentences the very troublesome little words can give the child a hard time. Parts of the verb "to be"—"is," "am," "are," "were"—are abstract, and therefore much harder to learn to use than words such as "run," "eat," and "sleep."

Just stop a minute and think about the word "is." The more you say it by itself, the funnier it sounds. However, this is one of our basic English words. Just by adding "is" to a phrase such as "that Daddy" changes it to "that is Daddy" and makes the child's speech sound more adult. The use of sentences makes our ideas and needs easier to understand and therefore more acceptable.

A child who is learning to use complete, correct sentences must learn that verbs have many forms, and each form has a special meaning. Through experience and listening to the speech around him a child learns that words change when being used to tell about different happenings: "I came home from school" tells us something different from "I will come home from school."

Before a child can develop this ability to change words in this way he must understand and learn about how time passes. "Yesterday," "today" (now), and "tomorrow" must mean something to him. This does not mean that he must know how to tell time by the clock but that he understands the meaning of past, present, and future. For many years it was thought that children with severely retarded development could never learn about time. They were called "today children." Supposedly yesterday or tomorrow meant nothing. Such an idea could easily become a "fact" when children were placed in institutions very young, had no stimulation, no education, nothing to look forward to but another day just like all days—nothing exciting to remember. It's no wonder these little ones said few words, if any. The early "speech lessons" were usually just learning to label a few basic things and needs, and certainly if it were true that yesterday and tomorrow held no meaning, how could the child possibly use the past or future tense of verbs!

It isn't easy for our children to learn the rules of grammar. For almost everybody the use of past and future tenses of verbs just seems to happen, but for developmentally retarded or disabled children this is difficult. Each step must be planned and carefully followed.

By studying many angles of each special child in a project a pattern seemed to show up upon which we could start to build a meaningful program. All very young children are concerned mainly with their own things, just themselves and their families. The child's concern for himself and where and how he moves himself is perfectly natural and provides a way to capture interest and attention. This block of activity is called Total Body Activity or TBA.

The child must learn to control his body activity by learning *what we move*—body parts, *where we move*—directions, and *how we move*—walk, run, hop, etc. We start teaching the child *to identify parts of his body*, using his own head first.

You say "nose," touch his nose, touch your nose, saying "nose" each time. Take the child's hand and guide it to touch his nose and your nose. Do this same thing with "eyes," "mouth," "ears," "chin," "hair," "teeth," "tongue," "neck." Don't forget to reward him.

"Tummy" is a good easy word. Use "hand," "finger," "thumb," "foot," "toes." Identifying joints seems to be a harder task, so hold back on "wrist," "elbow," "knee," "ankle." "Leg" and "arm" are not very easy.

Learning to help during undressing or dressing becomes easier as the child learns the names of body parts. "Put your foot in your pants" sounds so very simple, yet if the child does not know and identify that thing on the end of his leg as *his foot*, nor does he understand the words "in" and "out," "up" and "down," "over" and "under," "front" and "back," it is very hard for him to follow directions for managing clothing.

So we must teach the meaning of these words that tell us *directions*, such as "in" and "out." This is done with total body activities such as crawling through a short "tunnel." You can use a large carton, open at both ends, a barrel or oil drum, or a tunnel made of overturned chairs. All you need to do is show him what you expect him to do—do it yourself. Say "in" pointing to the tunnel, give him a little help getting *in*, then quickly get around to the other end, with a reward in your hands as you say "out." He really has no place to go but "out"—so he is sure to succeed.

A warning here: *do not use* the long cloth caterpillar-type commercial tunnel for this activity. It may be too scary. It's lots of fun later but can spoil the whole learning experience if used to start the idea of "in" and "out."

Now you can dream up a variety of ways to teach these direction words, using the total body: "in" and "out" of the bathtub, the car, a toy wagon, an entire room—"Go *in* the kitchen. Come *out* of the kitchen." Always reward success, using smiles, hugs, and praise instead of food as soon as possible.

Games to teach "up" and "down" and the other basic directional words are easily planned. Just remember always to *say* the word, clearly and pleasantly, as you are teaching the meaning.

Activities for *how* we move include walking or running, holding the child's hand and just saying, "Walk, walk, walk, walk," etc.

You might well wonder what all this has to do with learning about time and verbs. When the child learns to control his body, knows what he must move, where and how he moves, you use his body control to learn about *when* he did something.

He himself is totally involved in the action. You hand him a newspaper and say, "*Take* this to Daddy." Daddy receives the newspaper, says, "Thank you," then Mother says, "You *took* the newspaper to Daddy." After a few successful tries, you can expect him to imitate your direction. You say, "Take this newspaper to Daddy," then have the child imitate, "I take (or "will take") the newspaper to Daddy." When the child returns, say, "What did you do?" then say, "I *took* the newspaper to Daddy." Help him, reward him, and you'll get results. You can start to use the future tense by teaching "Tomorrow (or tonight) we will take the newspaper to Daddy." Please be sure you and Daddy have studied this together and planned an uninterrupted time to play the game.

When a child experiences something himself, learning is much easier, especially when he has Daddy and Mother all to himself, and they seem to be happy to be with him.

The use of the complete sentence should be a goal for every language-retarded child. True, there are some handicapped children who may never reach this stage of language development (see Chapter 14), but with carefully planned training many children can and will develop these abilities.

The goal for children with retarded development is to be as independent as possible and as an adult to have a job, to feel wanted, worthwhile, and have some purpose in his life.

In studying those young adults who have succeeded in a job setting, we have found that carrying on complex conversations is not the most important use of language. Getting ideas across comfortably is always very important.

Paying attention so they can listen very carefully is absolutely essential so directions can be followed—so job orders and assignments can be carried out. The main cause of failure in a job, beyond being grouchy or unpleasant, *is failing to follow directions*. It isn't easy for handicapped people to follow directions given too fast or in words that are hard to understand.

Our career training must include learning to ask questions, to ask for help when needed, like not understanding some directions or orders. Knowing how and when to ask a question, and not being afraid to ask for needed information, can make the difference between success and failure in holding a job. We owe it to each child to help avoid failures and frustrations.

The jobholder must be ready to ask, "What did you say?" comfortably when he is not sure he has understood directions, orders, requests, or demands. When he is unfamiliar with a cleaning agent or a piece of equipment he must ask, "What is this?" "How do I use it?" or "Is this soap?"

To ask a question, the speaker not only must be able to

use a complete sentence but must also learn to rearrange words into a question—for example, after he can say, "This is soap" he must learn to switch the words around to *ask*, "Is this soap?" This skill must be practiced and practiced until it comes very easily.

You can make up games that will help to frame questions. Dramatic play and role playing are good exercises to learn to ask appropriate questions. Learning to ask for help should begin as soon as a child can use words and continue throughout his education.

Up to this point we have been telling you about how children learn to *use* words, to make sentences. We have followed a pattern for the normal growth and development of language, with some references to problems that can interfere with the expected development.

Now we must look at what can be planned to help a child who does not follow the general pattern—a program that can be carried on at home or with very young children. Some of these plans are repeating what has already been talked about but are so necessary to help the child. We will go into more detail, trying to make it clearer and give you some alternatives. Remember, when one way doesn't work, you must try another way.

You have already read Chapter 9, "Saying Real Words That Mean Something." If your child is *saying*, comfortably, words that mean something, you can move along to *using* words in a more complex manner, making sentences, and asking questions.

You will need some pictures showing action, such as a man *painting* a house, Mother *shopping*, a person *pitching* a ball, a person *catching* a ball, a girl *jumping* a rope, a woman *cooking* or *baking*, a man *working*, *cutting* grass, someone *swimming*, or *riding* in a car. Be sure you use only

pictures of something your child has seen. It is very important to be sure your child has seen someone doing these
actions. You must not expect him to learn new words. He is
learning to *say* and *use* words he already knows about.

Show the most familiar pictures first. *Painting* is a very
good one to start with. Every child has seen someone with a
paintbrush in hand.

Let the child see the picture and say, "Man painting."
Then ask, "What is the man doing?"

You may only get an answer such as "pay-ee" or just
"pay." That's all right. He has the idea. Don't press him for
better sound yet. *The idea is the most important thing now.*
You go on like this:

"*What* is the man doing?"

"Pay-ee."

"That's right—painting." (If he does not say anything,
you say "painting.")

"*What* is the man painting?" (Say the word "painting"
with firmness. Hit the *t* hard.)

"House." (Or whatever it is.)

"That's right—good! *Painting his house. Who is painting* his *house*?"

"Man." (Or "Daddy.")

"Good—the man is painting his house." (Slowly please!)
"Now, you tell me, 'The man—' " Wait, he'll probably say
"man." "Is painting—" Wait—he'll say "pay-ee." "His house
—" Wait—he'll say "house." Reward him!

Always say the word for him *if* he shows signs of failure
to get the word out. Knowing just when to say a word for
your child after you have asked him to say it is a matter of
practice on your part.

The word "probe" is used to tell about a way you can
help a child say a word. Sometimes a child is all set to say

a word, and it just won't come out. So you help him *by probing*. This means you give him a start. It goes like this. You would say, "I'm the cookie monster! Now you say it— 'I'm the cookie m——.'" You say just the *m* sound of monster. Be very sure the child is looking at your mouth. If his lips come together to shape an *m*, reward him quickly. You might need to say, "I'm the cookie mon——," giving him most of the word. This is called a *probe* because you probe your way into getting the child's attention and spark his memory for the word sounds.

You can do this with familiar poems or songs such as

> Baa-baa black sh——
> Have you any w——?
> Ye—, sir, ye—, sir
> Three b—— full.

Always be sure to complete the word if the child does not do it himself, but keep trying.

The language story system for teaching children to make complete sentences and improving their grammar will be very effective if used carefully, following the directions exactly.

You must never demand a word to the point of the child showing signs of stuttering. Some children with Downs Syndrome are apt to start to stutter under too much pressure to say words. Be patient.

But you must not give the word to your child too easily or he'll soon find out he doesn't have to try hard.

If you have paid close attention to the rules for speech lessons, your child will try hard, and you will know when to give him the help he needs to succeed.

Go on doing the same thing with another picture. Two pictures a lesson are enough. Use the same picture for a day or so. Then add a new one. Be sure you keep the old one for comfort. Finish each lesson with the "old" pictures to be sure you stop with a success.

You should have at least six of these "action" pictures to work with.

Don't expect the child to put all these words together without help until several lessons are past. You will get quicker answers and better words if you don't push too hard. The words "the," "is," and "a" will come later.

If he says, "Man painting house," or "Da man paint house," he is doing very well.

When you feel he is doing pretty well you can go about it like this: Show the two pictures that he knows the best. Say, "Show me the picture of the man painting his house . . . . That right—good—the man is painting his house. Now you tell me about it." You may be quite surprised how much your child will give you from the picture. Do not ask a question that can be answered by just "yes" or "no." You want words put together. Questions satisfied by "yes" or "no" answers or head movement for "yes" or "no" are fine for learning to listen or for nonverbal children such as some cerebral-palsied or cleft-palate children.

Pick up the other picture and say, "Tell me about this." If he can't get started, help him, the same way you did on the first picture. Ask:

"*What* is he doing?"
"*Who* is doing it?"
"Tell me about it."

To respond to "Tell me about it" is a big jump for the child and it may take time. *Always help him if he needs it —never let him fail.*

Your child must always feel he is doing all right. It's a

hard thing to know when you are helping too much and not urging enough. You must feel your way along. Helping too much is better than to cause damage by allowing your retarded child to feel he can't do it or has failed to please you.

Now you can go on to all kinds of pictures to help him make sentences. Here are some of the pictures you can use:

A baby sleeping
A woman shopping
A boy running
A woman washing clothes
A woman ironing clothes
A woman making cake, pie, or cookies
A man smoking a pipe or cigarette
A baby eating dinner
A man buying gas or fixing a tire
A man driving a bus
Boys playing ball
A man shoveling snow

Good pictures of all these activities can be found in magazine advertisements. You will get pretty good at picking out pictures. Some calendars have good action pictures. Keep your eyes open for good pictures. Greeting cards often have very attractive pictures. (See page 204.)

Pictures of foods are good, and many can be found in magazines. The words easiest to start with are:

butter	milk	peaches
beans	mashed potatotes	peas
beer	meat	pizza
bacon	pie	pickle
banana	pop	potatoes

You can use these word pictures by saying, "Tom likes

pie," "Tom likes milk," "I like milk," etc. Use the favorite foods of different members of the family. "Daddy likes pizza," "Mother eats peaches," "Polly eats pickles." You can also use "I see ——," "I like ——," "I eat ——," or "I want ——."

Words with more than one syllable, like apples, hot dogs, coffee, ice cream, pizza, will usually come along without too much trouble after the first group of *b* words is learned. (Find reference on page 205.)

Many retarded children, especially children with Downs Syndrome, will say the first part of a word and clip off the rest of it, saying "bo" for "boat" or "cu" for "cut." They may also slur over the middle of a word. saying "ea-ing" for "eating." You should not worry about this until your child is saying lots of words freely and using them in the right way. If you fuss about details at first, you won't get very far. Remember we are after *usable* speech.

As your child moves along, making short sentences, you might notice that he does not use pronouns. He is less likely to say "mine" or "I" than to use his own name. Normal children do this for a while but move on to using pronouns quite easily.

The nouns and verbs used by children with retarded development are those that can be pictured, such as "A man is painting" (and the child will skip over "is"). These are the *concrete* words, words that can be pictured.

Conversation will be about things and events that are real; things that can be seen or actually experienced. These real things concern only the child at first, then his family.

Young children working together in a small group situation have a better opportunity to broaden their ideas beyond themselves. "He" and "she" will replace proper names after several months in a nursery or prekindergarten group.

Abstract words such as "love," "happiness," "sick," "truth," "funny," "yes," and "no" are difficult to find pictures for. Children can pick up the meaning of these words from cues in pictures such as facial expression or just by the tone of voice you use when talking about them.

A teacher with a small group can do this during circle time. The teacher has a colored card for each child with his name printed in bold carefully written manuscript. She holds up a name and says, "Tommy, is Tommy here?" If Tommy is absent, she shakes her head, says, "No, Tommy is *not* here—too bad," and looks sad. And, of course, if Tommy is here she says, "Yes, Tommy is here. Good morning, Tommy," and smiles—so does Tommy.

We can help children with retarded development become better acquainted with words and their use more readily by helping them to associate words with things they can see and handle. All children need to act with their thoughts and ideas. A large dollhouse with appropriate furniture is helpful in doing this.

Start with the dollhouse all set up, its furniture in place. Name the rooms and what we use them for: "Kitchen—we cook in the kitchen. Bedroom—we sleep in the bedroom."

Next, start with no furniture in place in the dollhouse and a box of furniture for just one room. The kitchen is the best place to start. Point to the kitchen. Say, "Kitchen—we cook in the kitchen." Pick up each piece of furniture in the box and name it: "This is a stove," "This is a table," and so forth.

Then let the child pick one thing at a time from the box and name it (help him). You say, "Kitchen—put it in the kitchen." Reward him when he puts the stove in the proper room. Reward him if he only starts to move his hand in the right direction, then guide his hand to the proper place.

Take a different room the next day. He may not be able to name all the furniture, so you must help him.

When he is acquainted fairly well with all the rooms, with your help, you can try a harder step.

Start with no furniture in the house and place about ten various pieces of furniture in front of him. Ask him to pick each one up, name it, and place it where it belongs.

Then ask him to tell you about it. For example, he selects a bed. He says, "Bed—the bed goes in the bedroom. Tommy sleeps in a bed." Reward him.

Without much pressure, he is producing some good sentences.

Always remember to be very patient, to make lesson time a fun time, and not be picky about little errors in the way some sounds are made—time enough later to work on special sounds that cause trouble.

At this point we want the child to feel comfortable about putting his ideas into words and sentences and to want to keep working with you because it is a happy time with you.

12

Some Sounds That Need Help

MANY DEVELOPMENTALLY DELAYED CHILDREN, particularly Downs Syndrome children, will use one vowel sound only. This is the *u* sound as in "up." They will use it in all words. They will say "mu" for "milk" or "mama," "wu" for "water," "ku" for "key" or "cut."

Some variety must be learned if other people are to understand your child.

When you are working with the *b, p,* and *m,* words, you will see a variety of these vowel sounds: *a* as in "baby," *a* as in "ball," *e* as in "me," *i* as in "bike" or "pipe." You might need to give your child some extra help by playing some special games.

A long *e* as in "whee" will pop out, sometimes while playing with a ball, rolling or tossing it. Make a project of playing this game. Use a large, rough-surfaced rubber ball. Every time you roll or throw the ball, use "whee" as if it were lots of fun. If your child has trouble catching—and he probably does—have him sit on the floor with his legs far apart so he can't miss. You sit a few feet away, and roll the ball gently to him. Start the ball quite near him so you will be sure he can catch it as it rolls toward him. Roll it back and forth and say "whee!" (and nothing else!) with each roll.

Oo is very easy to teach because you can "see" it, and most children will learn it quite early playing peek-a-boo. Also, when someone gets a little hurt, say, "Oo, oo, ouch" —and you might get both vowel sounds, *oo* and *ou*, as in "ouch."

When your child has control of a few vowel sounds, the rest will come along as he learns to say words. Remember, we are not working for perfect speech.

You will not need to go into detail and teach each sound to your child. He will learn by hearing and listening. Most likely he will learn the words as a whole. He will not learn "b-u-s" as three sounds—he will catch the whole word.

Breaking words down does not help a very young delayed child. Sometimes you can hold onto one sound to help him, but the whole word should be used. For example, try the word "apple." Downs Syndrome children and some brain-damaged children will often say "upple." Saying the word with an exaggerated A-pple can help. "Apple" can be very hard to say.

"Elephant" is a hard word, but many an *l* has been learned by dramatically holding on to the *el*—even though the rest of the word may not come out right. One of the best kindergarten teachers for handicapped children gets an *l* sound in a most unusual way. She uses a group of food pictures—bacon, beans, chicken, cheese, Jell-O, apple (with a bite out of it), milk. (These children all have speech—they have used all the *b* words and are *using* speech.) After each of these food words is used, she says, "Mm—dee-*l*icious," and it is never long before each little one is saying "dee-*l*icious" and making a good *l* sound whenever it is needed.

R, s, sh, th, v, amd *f* are so hard for many developmentally delayed children that they never do learn to say them very well. Taking these sounds out of words and working on them does not seem to help much. Playing a game, saying a poem, or singing a song that leads the child to imitate the sounds is the best way.

It is never too late to learn new sounds, and we should not stop trying to improve when usable speech has been achieved. A child of thirteen has been known to learn the sound *r* in "Mary" to replace "Ma-wy." The difficult *th* may be learned as an adult.

If your child never learns to say a good *r* sound (or *th* or *s*) don't nag him. You will only make him unhappy with the way he talks, and he has enough trouble without this added to his problems.

One little Downs Syndrome child has learned to talk very well. She has a fine vocabulary and uses good sentences. The day before a long-awaited trip to the circus, she greeted her teacher, saying, "We can hahdly wait till tomowwow, can we, Mit De Wode?" No *r*'s and no *s*'s. Her teacher would not change distorted sound for a correct, less joyful use of language. The little girl's happy contact through speech is what is important.

When you feel that your child is quite comfortable using a lot of words, you can help him "correct" some of the clipping and omitting of sounds. Be sure you don't make him feel he is doing something wrong. Make it a game.

Use the "painting" picture or the "eating" picture. Sit very close with your arm around the child, whisper the word "painting." Do it a few times to yourself and see what happens. All you really hear is "p-n-t." The *t* comes out quite strong.

To repeat any word correctly, a child must remember every sound in order. "P-a-i-n-t-i-n-g" is a lot to remember, so he goes just so far, perhaps to the first and second sounds, and stops. When you whisper, he hears and has to remember and say only two sounds, and he carries on to the *t*. The *ing* is lost at this point but that is nothing to worry about. If you get the *t* and hit it hard, you have really accomplished something. You whisper the whole word "painting" instead of just saying "paint" because that way you will say the *t* harder than if you just said "paint." Do the same thing with "skating." Use good pictures of someone painting or skating.

After a few lessons, using the whispering way, you can teach your child to pick up the final sounds of many words that he already uses but clips. Try this way with other words such as "boat," "bed," "bus." Whisper and hit that last letter very hard.

Be sure you do not try to do this until your child is comfortably using a lot of words. It is very important that he is able to use words easily and in the right places before you try to help him with the middle or end sounds in words.

We have been talking about how we can help handicapped children *say* troublesome sounds.

Voice problems need attention also. This means we must pay attention to how loud or soft, how high or low, and how pleasantly your child talks.

The "too loud" explosive burst of speech is very annoying to families and school groups. Sometimes children talk too loud because the entire family talks too loud. More often the child may talk too loud because he cannot control this loudness of his voice by his own listening. It is hard to teach him to speak softly, but it is very important to help him to speak in a gentle tone of voice. The example of your own gentle speech will help more than anything else.

If you can possibly use a tape recorder, make a recording

of a conversation with the child. Tape it as he talks, with no corrections or criticism. Be sure to have your conversation planned so you will get a good sample of your speech and your child's speech.

Play it back and do not cut down the volume. Let him hear how loud it is. You can help him notice the loud spots by acting startled or unpleasantly surprised whenever a loud spot occurs. Don't say anything—just act—be a ham! Reward him for pleasant speech frequently. Every now and then, when your child speaks softly, hug him and say, "You said that *so* nicely!" and maybe give him a treat.

Then make another recording and urge him to "talk as I do."

If the recorder has a monitor on it, show your child how the light band fans out and how you want to keep it in that one little spot. Sometimes this works like magic. Even if he cannot hear himself, he can "see" himself talk too loudly.

Try using hand puppets. You have one on your hand, and the child has one on his hand. Make up a conversation, and when the child talks too loudly, quickly put the puppet's "hands" over his ears. Your child will take this "correction" from the puppet with less resentment than he will take it from you.

Using hand puppets is also very relaxing and helpful in improving speech output. A child who is inclined to tighten up or stutter will carry on if the puppet instead of himself is doing the "talking."

You will find you, too, will be more relaxed with a puppet in your hand "talking" for you.

Don't start using puppets, however, until your child is talking. You need his full attention in the learning days. Use puppets as helpers to "talk better."

The child who talks too softly to be readily heard is

usually the shy child with other problems. Being with a *small* group of children will help the shy child.

Using a tape recorder and puppets will help here also. The child's attention must be drawn to the need to speak louder. Use the same methods as those given for the child whose voice is too loud. Let him listen to a recording of his conversation, watch the monitor during a recording, and play with puppets, only this time, when the voice is too low, cup the puppet's hand around an ear.

Some types of handicapped children are monotones when they try to sing and show very little variety in pitch during regular conversation. Very little can be done to help these children sing or hum or carry a tune, but the speaking voice can be improved.

Here again dramatic play with hand puppets is a big help. Monkey hand puppets are used, and the game is called "Monkey Sees, Monkey Does." The child's puppet must do just what the teacher's puppet does.

Cock the puppet's head to one side and, waving a "hand," say "Hell-o," accent on the first syllable. The child must imitate this.

Then cock the puppet's head to the other side and say "Hell-o," heavy accent on the second syllable. The "monkey" is more apt to imitate the melody in your voice than the child would without the puppet.

Continue doing this, using many *simple* expressions, such as "How are you?" "I am fine." "How's your mother?"

Be sure you exaggerate the melody in your voice and have fun in doing it.

Some children seem to "talk through their noses." This nasal speech happens because some sounds that need to bounce off the palate do not "sound off" properly. It is very difficult to retrain a child with this problem. The best way is to have him imitate a good example with a hand puppet.

When you plan your dramatic play with hand puppets for a child with nasal speech, try to avoid words ending in *ng* such as "bang," "sang," "sung," "wing."

Ella Jenkins has recorded some special music that is very useful in helping handicapped children with special sounds. The recording has many bands of a wide variety of rhythms and tunes. "Taboo" and "Moon Don' Go" are the tunes with a game approach that are specially good. Many children will just listen and pop out a correct sound now and then as they listen to the recording. It is fun to watch a child as he listens to Ella Jenkins set the patterns for him to imitate. Very often lips and jaw will move almost shaping the sounds that would mimic Miss Jenkins. "Taboo" is easier to follow. "Moon Don' Go" is rather tricky. One big thing in favor of using these recordings is the interest they hold for older handicapped children. It's not "baby stuff," and it's fun to do. (See Appendix L for where to buy these recordings. Also see suggestions in Appendix D for using cassette recordings.) As you will be using only these two bands, "Taboo" and "Moon Don' Go," record each one three times in succession so you can do the games three times without having to relocate the band on the recording to get a repeat, and break into the child's attention by reaching for the record player arm and likely making a squawking sound when the needle misses the right spot! Having the game repeated three times allows children in a group to take turns being the leader.

13

Conversation and Manners

GOOD MANNERS SHOW through the way a person asks for or tells or says something. Letting someone else know how you feel about someone or something is very important. Getting what you want by asking for it is also very important.

For the child with retarded development, good manners are of utmost importance. Adults are apt to judge a child good or naughty, rude or polite, very quickly by the first thing the child says in his presence.

If a friend comes to your house and rings the doorbell, and your child can answer and say, "Hello, please come in," or, "Please sit down," or "I'll call my mother," rather than yowling, "Ma, someone's here," the well-mannered greeting helps your friends accept the child.

All children should have good manners, but your special child should have *excellent* manners. This helps all children with retarded development to be accepted and liked by everybody. You must set a good example yourself.

You must teach your child by acting out these situations. Make it a game. Go outside and ring the doorbell or have a brother or sister do it. Go through the whole business of greeting.

Practice quietly calling to someone in another room and telling a member of the family that guests have arrived.

Here is a list of "good manners" speech you must try to teach your child.

ANSWERING THE DOORBELL. A child should not be permitted or expected to answer the door by himself in a large city where there are more strangers than friends. Someone should go to the door with him and stand by to handle the situation should an unidentified stranger be present.

In places where few strangers might come to the door and the parents feel it is safe to allow the child to open the door, the child should be taught to say, "Just a minute, please, my mother is coming" and *close the door.*

ANSWERING THE TELEPHONE. The very young retarded child can be a help to Mother by answering the phone and just saying, "Hello, Mommy's coming." Practice all telephone manners on a toy telephone. Be sure to teach him to come get you right away.

PLEASANT CONVERSATION. Practice this in a game called "Happy Talk." Do it at the dinner table where everyone in the family can play. Everyone takes a turn in saying something pleasant. Mother can start by saying, "Daddy, John was a big help today. He took out all the old newspapers for me." Then it's Daddy's turn. He could say, "Mother, this is good stew." Then it's sister's turn. She could say, "Thanks, John, for taking out the papers. Saved me a job." John could say, "I like carrots like this." And soon you will be surprised how much this game will do for all the members of your family. Saying nice things is much healthier than saying things that are unpleasant. Help your special child when it is his turn to say something happy. You can play "Happy Talk" in the car, saying something nice about pretty or interesting things. Your child needs to be helped to say pleasant things. It will help him to get along with people.

ACCEPTING A COMPLIMENT. Even many grown-ups are flustered over a compliment, and a child with retarded development will be more so. A little practice can make it quite easy to accept. Teach your child to say "Thank you" when someone says something nice to him, or, "Thank you, I like it very much, my aunt gave it to me" when a friend admires something he is wearing.

WHAT IS GOOD SUBJECT MATTER FOR CONVERSATION? Work with your child to help him make conversation. Teach him some good stock questions, such as, "What did you do today?" "Did you see the ball game on TV yesterday?" (TV programs are always good subjects for openers.) "How are your violets doing?" You should coach your older child before he meets people. Give him a start to a good conversation. After a while he will be able to do it without help.

Grown-ups will often talk about things at home in front of children and are horrified to hear the child repeat it to others. Your child with retarded development can use very little judgment in deciding what is not to be repeated. The safest way to avoid this embarrassment is not to discuss private or controversial affairs where he can hear you.

BAD LANGUAGE. Children with retarded development usually have a limited social circle. *Their patterns of language will be set by you*; a few close friends, immediate families, and television are also strong influences. These children seldom gang up on a street corner or at a soda fountain. Children with Downs Syndrome, particularly, will copy anything they hear after they have started to talk. Parents must be very careful about using rough language. Every child experiments with swear words at one time or another. Your special child will try these words only if he hears them quite frequently.

USING ACCEPTABLE WORDS FOR GOING TO THE TOILET. The words that come most easily to a child when he wants to go to the toilet are not the most socially acceptable. These three can be used: "potty," which is quite easy to say; "bathroom," which is a little harder; and "toidey," which is very hard to say. Insist that your child use one of these words. "Potty" should be one of the first words you teach your child to say. Very few children are ever successfully toilet trained until they start to talk or learn some acceptable gesture to let you know they want to go to the bathroom. Teaching your child to say "potty" is very important, and will help you in training him. (See Chapter 9.)

It is not difficult to teach your child to "sign" the word for potty if he does not say the word. The "sign" is much better than resorting to a quick grab at himself and crossed knees.

If you teach your child to use the "sign" for potty, always say "potty" the moment you see the sign. This will help him to learn to say "potty."

ASKING QUESTIONS. Your language-delayed child may get what he wants by pointing or by pulling you to what he wants. He may "act out" what he wants, and you learn to figure out what he means. As he gets older he may name what he wants, such as "cookie." He will go on to say, "Tom, cookie," then "Me, cookie," or "Wanna cookie." When your child can say "Me, cookie," or "Me, milk," you can teach him to say, "Milk, please." It is quite hard for many handicapped children to say, "May I please have a cookie?" It is wonderful if your child can learn to ask a question that way; but with so much to learn, it seems hardly necessary to make a big fuss about it. A pleasant manner and "please" are quite enough for your child at this time.

TELEPHONE MANNERS. You should not allow your child to answer your phone until he is able to say words. "Mommy's coming" is all right for helping Mother. Your child can learn to answer very simply by saying, "Hello, this is Eddie." You will have to practice this with him. Teach him to wait after he has said, "Hello, this is Eddie," and listen so he can find out who is calling. He should learn to say his name over the phone as soon as the call is answered. It should go like this: Phone rings, Eddie answers, "Hello, this is Eddie." He listens and hears, "This is Aunt Betty." "How are you?" he replies. If it is a stranger calling, it should go like this: Phone rings, "Hello, this is Eddie." He must wait and listen: "Hello, Eddie, this is Mr. Brown. May I speak to your father, please?" "I'll call him" or, if Father is not at home, "I'll call my mother."

If adults watch their telephone manners, the child will get along fine. But if you start out by saying "Where's your father?" you may get a very frank answer!

USING A PLEASANT VOICE. A loud, sharp, or monotonous voice is not very pleasant. A voice that is too soft can hardly be heard. Some children with retarded development have an explosive type of speech.

All these voice problems usually do not offend the ears of the *speaker*. He must be made aware of the unpleasantness of the sounds he produces before he can help himself to correct the problem.

Detailed instructions for helping the child by the use of a tape recorder are found in Chapter 12.

The deep, husky voice of the Downs Syndrome child will not change much, but that is not important. It's *what* he says and *how pleasantly* he says it that matters.

Whatever the voice problem, remember that the goal is pleasant, polite, gentle, and understandable speech.

Children with retarded development try very hard to please adults. As they reach their teens they will usually agree rather than argue a point, whether it favors them or not.

Parents and teachers should be extremely careful in questioning a teen-ager about some unpleasantness. These teen-agers are highly suggestible and will actually agree to anything they think you expect them to say. They can be led to accuse or defend themselves or each other. They are not malicious liars nor can it be said that they are untruthful. "Small wars" can be avoided if adults will be cautious about "putting words in their mouths." If a problem comes up in a group of children with retarded development, solve it yourself. Ask guarded questions if you can't avoid doing so, but don't lead one of these trusting children into a false situation.

Instead of asking, "Did you see John hit Sharon?" say, "Tell me what happened," and *take time to listen.*

Your handicapped child is usually very anxious to do things on his own, but don't send him to the store or on an errand to strangers until you are sure he is ready to make such a trip alone. There is always some unkind or unknowing person who could make your child very sad. Be *very* sure he can say what he needs to say or can safely deliver a written note.

Your own manners, gentle speech, and relaxed attitude will do more to teach your child than any lessons you could possibly plan. Always set a good example yourself and always remember to reward your child for good behavior and manners.

14

Another Way for the Child Who Does Not Learn to Talk

The Use of Communication Boards and Total Communication

IT IS HOPED THAT MOST CHILDREN will learn to talk. If your child does not continue to progress in using words, another way must be used to help him let his needs be known. For many years we just wouldn't give up trying to teach developmentally retarded children to talk, even when all signs seemed to point to the need to try another way. Many of the things we do to help a child to talk have been learned from the ways used to teach a deaf child to talk. And we must admit that we made some mistakes in expecting to get spoken words from all handicapped children.

Now we know that some children with or without any hearing problems just are not able to produce a meaningful spoken word, yet these children have needs and ideas that should be expressed. We must learn to watch for that point of true frustration when the words just will not come and the ideas are bursting to come out. Before reaching this frustration point, the child will try to let you and the whole world know he is very unhappy—naughty behavior, defiance, destruction, anger, striking out, spitting, biting, or he may just cry—all these are signs of frustration and unhappiness.

Have you ever been around an older person who has had a stroke and whose right side is paralyzed? Speech is gone, and people say, "He has had a behavior change—just not the same person he used to be." If you have been around a stroke patient who has been an active and successful person, you would learn quickly what real frustration can do to anyone's behavior!

So it is with our little ones who can't get words to work for them. We must use another way to get those ideas across before behavior gets in the way so badly you are about to give up the whole game.

Some children are unable to produce verbal language because of severe problems such as cleft lip and palate, which may include damage to nerve endings of the tongue, lips, and soft palate. Some children remain silent because it's the easy way out of trouble, like being shushed too much for being noisy. We call this type of silence "the shushing syndrome." Sad to say, we still have far too many badly managed institutions where a quiet cottage is a "good" cottage, and the poor tykes are shushed when even the joy of being alive gets the upper hand and squeals of delight fill the air. Children's vocal play is necessary. Please understand, there is a difference between fun noise and pandemonium.

A child with retarded development in a large, loving family sometimes is so loved, waited on, and all wants are anticipated so he has little need to talk. Overly protective parents can do the same thing to a handicapped child. They seem to smother the child's need to talk. Many children with cerebral palsy may have so many problems with coordination that they are unable to make the difficult movements necessary to speak.

By the time a child with retarded language development reaches seven or eight years of age he should have at least a minimal spoken vocabulary of about twenty-five single words. Most developmentally retarded children are using two-word combinations or speaking in simple sentences at seven or eight years of age. Generally these children understand many more words than they say, unless a hearing loss is involved.

In addition the child may be using some gestures of his own making that are not always understood by others, and this can be frustrating to him. A planned system of gestures to be understood by others is called *signing* or *total communication*. We'll talk about this system after telling you about another means of "talking" and that is by the use of *communication boards*.

Communication Boards

Rather than waiting until frustration starts to get the upper hand and hanging on to the hope that someday he will talk, let's give your child another way of talking. Hang on to that hope and keep trying but wait a while until another way has been tried and your child gets a feeling of success through a different way.

A communication board is no more than a cue board which contains pictures or printed words of common, everyday things that your child may want or need. The child learns to point to the picture of what he wants to "say" and you don't need to struggle with the game of "guess what."

Begin with only two or three pictures at a time so that the child will not fail to let you know what he is "saying." The pictures used depend upon the individual child. Cut out pictures or take snapshots of common objects such as a glass or a cup of milk, a toilet, a TV, or a cookie and mount them on a piece of cardboard or light plywood.

Sit close beside your child. Be sure he is comfortable, feet touching the floor, sitting at a low table or beside you on the sofa. Have pictures of a cookie and a glass of milk in your lap and an easel of some kind (see Appendix C) on· the table. Have a glass with a little milk in it and a small, not too brittle cookie set to one side where you can reach it easily. Placing the real milk or cookie on another chair where the child can't see it would be better if you can manage it this way. Put one picture against the easel and say "cookie"—don't say anything else. Then put the other picture against the easel and say "milk." Don't say anything else.

Now you will show him what you want him to do. Say, "Listen—look" as you reach to point at the picture of the milk and say, "Show me milk." Take his hand and guide it toward the picture. Do the same thing, pointing to the cookie.

Now you're going to ask him to "show me the milk" as he reaches toward the right picture (remember two pictures are in front of him to choose from), quickly say, "Milk!—right!—good!" and give him a sip of milk from the handy cup beside you.

Do the same thing using the cookie picture. *Do not let him fail.* Take his hand if he is confused and lead his hand toward the right picture—praise him and give him the reward even if you did most of it. He must get the feeling of "I did it," and he'll get this feeling when he knows he is pleasing you and being nicely rewarded. Help a little less each time, and before very long he will follow the command without your hand helping him. As the idea seems to catch on, you can stop rewarding him every time and reward only every other time, and then after five or six successful pointings.

When you know that he understands this step, ask him to show you what he wants. Say, "What do you want—milk or cookie—show me." Now he must select the right picture to tell you what he wants. If you just say, "What do you want?" he might want both! Then you would not be sure he understood the picture game you have been playing.

Remember to use only useful items that he knows and will need in his everyday experience or life. For example:

Mother	go	milk
Daddy	drink	water
I (picture of self)	sad (a sad face)	cookie
eat	happy (a happy face)	toilet
sleep	potty	TV

Be very sure each picture has been learned before adding more.

When the child has learned to express some of his most basic needs this way with pictures, you can make up a permanent board, covering each picture with plastic spray or other sealer such as transparent contact paper.

Since communication boards should be kept at a reasonable size, not too big and hard to manage, it will be necessary to make several boards, such as one for different times of the day or for special occasions. Picture boards may be used in many ways. For example, some children with retarded development will learn to read printed words with pictures.

When the child is reading the words on the picture cards, it is time to try to see if he can read the words without the pictures. It's a big step from pointing to a familiar picture to pointing to a printed word without the help of a picture.

You will need a set of pictures with the matching words on separate cards. Before you challenge the child to find the right word at the sound of your voice, practice matching the words to the pictures, then matching the pictures to the word. Start easy, don't use too many words at one time. Three pairs of pictures and words to start with are plenty. You can make up quite a large collection of good small pictures with matched printed words by cutting up some of the prereading primers or by making your own printed word cards.

When the child can match either way, by seeing the picture first and finding the printed word or the other way around, by seeing the printed word first and then finding the picture, it's time to try to use just the printed words. Many severely handicapped children may not get to this level. Some will learn to use quite a few words without pictures, and some will learn to recognize and use many words, including parts of speech other than just names of things and people. Some handicaps delay a child's development so severely that it seems that no progress could possibly be made. It is very important to try (and not stop trying) to reach a child's potential, but it is also very important not to push a child so hard that he feels constant failure and frustration and shows it by being very unhappy.

(Personal note from Mrs. Molloy: I shall always be grateful to Dr. Paul Moore for a most profound lesson in philosophy for teaching. He was talking to a parents' group about the problems our children face in learning to communicate. One father asked, "How do we know when to quit trying?" Dr. Moore answered, "The person who succeeds in any task, has tried just one more time than those who have failed." So we never stop trying, but we must be careful to avoid the frustration that comes with too much demanding. It's better to keep trying to find another way.)

This is what communication boards are all about—another way to keep trying, and with each new try we learn new and better ways to keep going, no matter how slow the pace may be.

Communication boards using only words open whole new worlds when the child is fortunate enough to learn to recognize whole batteries of words and to make sentences. Always we must remember the basic purpose of communication: the receiving and giving of ideas, the exchange of ideas. Handicapped children who do not develop a skill to use spoken words will vary in their ability to use a communication board system, just as all children vary from poor to good performance in any task. Some excellent work is being done at Ontario Crippled Children's Center in Toronto, Canada, to expand greatly the use of communication boards for people who do not use spoken language and are severely physically handicapped.

Among our handicapped children are many cerebral-palsied children whose potential is never reached because of the severe problems of communicating, and many of these children have normal or gifted intelligence. Specific instructions for developing a communication board for cerebral-palsied children can be found in an article by T. McDonald and A. Schultz, "Communication Boards for Cerebral Palsied Children" (see page 216).

Total Communication or a Gestural Language

For many years deaf people have "talked" with their hands. This could be done by using a single movement of hands and fingers for each letter of the alphabet and spelling out each word. Needless to say, if you cannot spell, this system is lost for you, and of course it is very slow and laborious.

Another system used for many years is made up of gestures or signs that mean whole words or even whole ideas. This system is much quicker and actually is fun. *Total communication* is the term used to define gestural language combined with spoken words and facial expressions. Sometimes you hear the system called *signing*. *Signing* is gestural language. If it is combined with spoken words, it is called *total communication.*

If a child is able to use his hands and imitate body movements, he should be able to learn gestural language. For a long time, just the gestures were used. Recently, spoken words were added to the gestures by educators of deaf children, and it worked very well. This system is called total communication or combined communication. This means that while teaching the child gestures the proper words are said at the same time by the teacher. This method works with speech-handicapped children who can hear, as well as it does for deaf children.

When you feel your child understands many spoken words (and you can tell when he follows directions spoken to him) and you are beginning to notice signs of frustration when you are working trying to get that first precious spoken word that just won't pop out, it's time to try another way.

We all use our hands while talking. Just try to talk to someone for any length of time and keep your hands still. You have undoubtedly been using gestures while talking to your child right along, such as a beckoning with your hand meaning, "Come to me," or placing a finger to the lips as a "hush" sign; we all use these common signs, and their meaning is understood by almost everybody.

Teaching the child with retarded development a gesture system must be done in a structured way. It is not a hit-or-miss idea. It is a system that must be learned by the child and by each person who will be receiving his message. You will need a book or a manual to teach this system. Study the book carefully so you will have some idea what it is all about. When you feel you have a good idea what you will be doing, you are ready to start. Two excellent books have been published recently: *Talk with Your Hands*, Vols. I and II, written and illustrated by David O. Watson (see Appendix H).

So let's start to teach your child to communicate by *signing*. Choose five everyday words that you are sure the child understands. Words which are the most common as well as those easy to make with the hands should be attempted first. It has been found that words such as "eat," "sleep," "mother," "father," "drink," "potty," "want," and "I" are a few of the best starter words. Another guideline is to choose those words which you think are most important for the child to learn.

One of the big advantages of a total communication (signing) system is that verbs can be learned almost at once. Also a child does not need to carry around anything extra like a communication board in order to let his needs be known. One of the disadvantages is that those people with whom the child wishes to communicate must understand the gestures that he is using. However, the rate at which most handicapped nonverbal children learn gestures or signs makes it realistic for their families to learn the signs at the same time. It doesn't do much good for a child to learn a set of signs at school and not be able to use them at home because members of the family have not learned them.

The best way to teach gestures or to teach anything is to choose a specific time of the day for a lesson and plan the time so you won't be interrupted. Just don't answer the telephone.

Always say the word you are signing. Use real objects such as a glass of milk or other beverage that he or she likes. Rather than teaching the "glass of milk" at first, teach the word "drink." Say the word "drink" and use the sign and then give the child a drink of the milk. Start using pictures with the object or action as soon as a few signs are learned. Using pictures is important because it is a good way to test the child to find out how much he has learned without imitating you. Show the child the picture, say the word, and make the sign at the same time. Encourage the child to do what you do. At first you may have to help him place his hand in the right way. Help him as much as he needs to be helped so he will not fail. Do not expect perfect imitation right away. It is not easy, but it is fun. Just as a child must practice with careful help to learn to talk, he also must practice with careful help to "talk with signs."

We have found that children enjoy signing in small groups. A family or class learning to sign together seem to help one another. Just the fact that the "talking" people are doing the same thing that the nontalking child is doing is a big boost for morale. The first attempt at getting an idea across by gestures and signs should be praised immediately.

Some children will seem to catch on very fast to the first dozen or more signs. Slow down and use these signs carefully before adding too many too quickly. When the list gets longer and remembering and selecting the right sign becomes hard, the rate of progress may slow down. You can expect this, so don't allow yourself or your child to become frustrated and decide it's too difficult. Just slow down and work hard with the comfortable signs and add new signs only when you feel sure it won't be confusing.

When you start to plan to teach your child to sign, a few things should be remembered: Don't wait too long to use signing. Start when you feel your child is making very little, if any, progress in trying to use words. It will be easier to teach the first sign to be learned if you choose a sign that requires only one very simple hand movement, such as "drink" or "eat." It is always important to remember to give your child every chance to do it right, to succeed, to get that wonderful feeling of "I did it."

Select the first words to be signed from very familiar things or actions:

Foods such as:	milk
	banana
	apple
	cookie and other favorites
Action words:	drink
	go
	sleep
	eat
	want
	come
Important words:	potty
	more
	happy

sad
hurt
no
yes

Always help the child to succeed. Place his hands in the right position if necessary and say the word at the same time. It goes like this:

1 You make the sign, saying the words at the same time.
2 Help the child place his hands to make the sign, say the word, and quickly again make the sign yourself, saying the word again.
3 Praise the child immediately.

Be aware that a slowdown will come, so be prepared for it and don't give up; just change your pace and strengthen the words already learned.

Keep up the lessons to learn to use words but don't push too hard. Signing, total communication, is another way to "talk." Children grow and change and surprise us with something we thought would never happen every now and then.

15

Children with Downs Syndrome

A BABY HAPPIER OR CUTER than a Downs Syndrome baby is hard to find. These very special children, if they are healthy, seem to come into the world contented and loving. If loved in return, well treated—not roughed up—and stimulated very early in life, they grow up happy, cooperative and capable of achieving skills that provide lifetime occupation, contentment, and a strong feeling of worthwhileness.

Not all children with Downs Syndrome are alike. For many years any child labeled *Mongoloid* was considered practically a total loss and treated as such. Most were placed in institutions right after birth and often forgotten or considered dead. They were placed in cribs, and because they were "so good" and demanded so little attention, they just lay there, unstimulated, not played with. Most of them died of pneumonia early in life, a few surviving until the early teens, and a few living a long life. Since the discovery of the *wonder* drugs, pneumonia is not the killer it once was.

Small wonder that these crib-bound children didn't try to walk until five years of age, or try to say any words until seven years of age, if then. They had no chance to explore, no need to move because they saw nothing beyond the range of the row of cribs. No effort was made for toilet training.

Doctors learned very little about these children except from reports from institutions.

Doctors don't like defeat any more than anyone else does, and to deliver a baby with Downs Syndrome and have the sad task of telling the parents is a very, very difficult job. Doctors don't deliver a Downs Syndrome baby very often and are usually just as shocked as the parents. Until the early 1960s most doctors were taught that such a child would never learn anything, never talk, so advised the parents to "put the baby away—and forget about it." Some doctors find it too difficult to tell the parents and put the inevitable day off as long as possible, even long after the parents are very sure something is wrong. Doctors suffer disappointments too.

In some places institutions will not admit an infant with Downs Syndrome. If the parents apply for admission, usually upon the advice of a doctor, foster home placement is arranged for, as it is known that these special little ones thrive in family living.

All the blame for not keeping the Downs Syndrome baby at home must not always be placed upon the doctor. Some families have problems that make separation necessary, and we must all be charitable in our thinking and attitude about the decision any family makes. Some children would be much better off in a good foster home. It's not always rejection of the child that leads to placement away from home. Serious health problems, family problems, such as loss of a parent, surely should not draw or deserve unkind criticism.

Downs Syndrome children are not all alike—far from it.

Intelligence may vary from very profound retardation to the normal range. A few Downs Syndrome children do function in the normal range. The average intelligence of Downs Syndrome children is just under half that of normal children. This means that the average healthy Downs Syndrome child will likely be capable of using judgment, making decisions, and communicating, very much like an eight- or ten-year old when adult years are reached. Downs Syndrome children will grow socially several more years than any IQ test will predict. We don't have a reliable measure for true social growth.

The very few Downs Syndrome children who have matured in the normal range of intelligence, and those who reach the so-called educable range, run into serious problems of social acceptance because of their appearance. Cosmetic surgery has been successful in enabling these luckier children to lead a more normal life.

Downs Syndrome children who have had happy stimulating babyhood days will very often score quite high on IQ tests until about three or four years of age, then they seem to level off, and the scores drop.

With the introduction of early infant intervention programs, starting intensive prescriptive therapeutic teaching as young as six weeks of age, indications are that children with developmental disabilities, especially Downs Syndrome children, will be capable of functioning at a higher level than previously predicted.

The Downs Syndrome baby needs intensive stimulation as early as possible.

Downs Syndrome children have some characteristics that are unique and identify them as Downs Syndrome children. We will concern ourselves here only with the differences that affect learning to communicate (those referred to in Chapter 6).

We talked about difficulties with tongue control. (See page 59.) The Downs Syndrome tongue is usually rough-textured, fissured, and hard to control, but some are just as smooth as a normal tongue. The voice tends to be husky, very likely due to texture changes in the voice box. Some of the huskiness often disappears in the upper teen years.

Many children with Downs Syndrome must be treated continually for ear infections which accompany colds. This problem is so persistent in some of the children that they must be treated every three months or even more frequently by a specialist. The continuation of a middle-ear infection can cause permanent damage to hearing. Some children respond very well to medication, others require additional treatment. One medical procedure consists of inserting plastic tubes into the eardrum to prevent breaking of the drum as well as the spreading of further infection.

Ear infections left untreated can be *very* serious. A child who has frequent ear infections usually has a loss of hearing that varies from day to day. The constant change in the way sounds are heard can delay speech and language development considerably more than is expected with retarded development. You could say the child has good and bad days. On the bad days he is missing important language-learning opportunities that may not be there tomorrow. Patience and proper medical management is needed when your child does not seem to respond to sound and speech.

Our children with Downs Syndrome mimic very readily. They seem to "see and do." They can imitate a model given to them very easily—and if rewards are used freely, quite a vocabulary can be built. This sounds very easy; but it is also dangerous, because the words are usually parrot talk and have little meaning in true language production. They must unlearn some words before *using* them meaningfully.

The same thing can happen because they mimic in a "hear and do" fashion. This can result in a very serious problem called "scribble speech." The child will mimic long chains of jargon, in perfect imitation of maybe a telephone conversation, using the same melody, pitch, pauses but *not* one single meaningful word. The first time the little one does this, it is hilariously funny—everybody laughs—the child loves the dramatic success and does it again—and will repeat the performance joyfully when asked, "Show Grandma how we talk on the phone." Once in a while a real word might be included, especially if it's a "song-and-dance act."

This scribble speech is practically impossible to stop so the child can use real words with meaning. Don't allow it to get started, as much fun as it is. The author recalls being entertained many times with "Show Mrs. M. about Hound Dawg"—and all the jargon and gyrations were great imitations, with only "Hown Dawg" coming through loud and clear. It took quite a while for the child to unlearn this meaningless achievement.

We must teach our children with Downs Syndrome meaningful, useful speech and language.

We can build upon mimicry just so far, and then we must demand appropriate word usage. We can encourage the Downs Syndrome child to "see and do," then to "say." So it goes like this:

See—do—*say*
Hear—do—*say*

You will follow the same steps talked about in Chapter 9 with some added precautions.

Downs Syndrome children will develop a stutter very quickly if they feel too much pressure to get words out. The pressure can come from being hurried, if parents get too anxious for results or impatient when the child is struggling inwardly to find the word he wants and then struggling to say the word. The same is true if too much pressure or importance is attached to making gains too fast in teaching. Give the child time to get his ideas across. Give him a little help but be very careful that he does not feel any impatience on your part.

Placing too much demand for speedy responses, changing the pace of any activity too quickly or without ample warning results in the well-known so-called stubborn spells you see so often in our Downs Syndrome children. The flow of movement is interrupted, and the child can't cope with it, so he will just plain quit or maybe throw himself on the floor and refuse to move. The more pressure put upon him to move, the more dug-in he becomes.

You can break up the reaction sometimes by a very exciting alternative such as, "Here comes the ice-cream man." This is a very weak solution and more of a bribe than a solution. *Prevention* is the best solution.

Don't make sudden demands, unless of course danger is involved. All households get hectic at times, with a big rush to beat the clock, but your little child with Downs Syndrome can't handle that confusion. Give yourself time, plan your time, so a more peaceful, serene atmosphere surrounds your family. It's good for everybody.

If you are to leave the house at 2:30 P.M., give your child at least a 10-minute warning. "In a few minutes we will go. When you finish get your coat." Or you might need to say —especially if the child is only half through what he is doing—or watching a TV program, "It's almost time to go. So, turn off the TV now. Get your coat, then we'll go." This may sound like you are giving in too easily. You are not.

You are preventing undesirable behavior and very upsetting scenes. Fortunately the Downs Syndrome children outgrow the stubborn reaction if they have not used it over a long time. They may resort to a sort of sulking behavior, or overshyness when the pace is too demanding.

The old literature tells us the Mongoloid children, if they did say a few words, would not use more than nouns, just naming words, would not use verbs, nor could they understand anything about time. Yesterday and tomorrow held no meaning. They were referred to as "today children."

We know that's all rather silly today. Our Downs Syndrome children, if started on the right path very early in life, will use all the parts of speech, good sentence structure, and project in time. And because they can learn to project in time, they can use correct verb tenses.

They may stay in the telegraphic stage of sentence structure longer than other children. We must remember we are talking about the average or above average Downs Syndrome child. The more handicapped Downs Syndrome child will progress more slowly and might not do too well in good sentence structure.

Here are a few things to remember when you are working with your Downs Syndrome little one.

> Don't allow mimicry stunts to get the upper hand.
> Don't pressure. Give plenty of time for responses.
> Watch weight. Don't let your child get chubby. A chubby child may be cute but will be a just plain fat adult.
> Do keep the child active. Learn to swim, to climb, to skate, to dance, to bowl, to hike. Have fun.
> Don't roughhouse with your child. Your child with Downs Syndrome will be just as kind and gentle as he is treated.
> Don't tease—most teasing is mean and not understood as somebody else's fun.

Do follow all the lessons in this book used for other handicapped children.

Do watch your own articulation. Downs Syndrome children often clip off the last sound in a word—like saying "pain-" for "paint." Hit that last *t* hard when you say that word—or any other word with a hard sound at the end.

Do be patient, the child needs time to process what he wants to say.

Do work hard on teaching your child to pay attention and to follow directions. This can make the difference between holding a job and not holding a job.

Do teach your child to ask for help and to say, "I don't understand," or "I don't get it—please say it again." He may not have heard it all, or it may be coming at him too fast. Just asking politely will usually slow down the speaker.

Children with Downs Syndrome have a delightful sense of humor. They see the point of riddles or jokes readily. Their chuckles and laughter are contagious.

Downs Syndrome adults can have very happy and useful lives if they are carefully trained for appropriate jobs with interested employers. They can do an excellent job in geriatric-care facilities as assistant aides. They have patience, a happy attitude, and are dependable. The same is true for working in child care, especially in day-care centers for handicapped little ones. The employer *must* understand this special adult and be willing to invest some time in additional training. Our schools train students with this job potential, but each job has some unique demands that the new employee must be taught to meet.

Custodial or maintenance assistance is another job possibility. Our Downs Syndrome adults can usually hold their jobs because they have such happy dispositions, are fun to be with, are patient and willing to stick with a tedious task.

We must be very realistic about job expectations. The placement with a community-interested employer will be satisfactory if:

1 The employer understands and wants the special worker.
2 You as parents are willing to accept with dignity and pride a job that, although menial by social standards, is done with pride and excellence.
3 You encourage your working adult to talk about his job with pride. He needs to feel wanted and worthwhile.
4 You play games that require following directions. Following directions is the key to holding a job.

Should the time ever come when a boarding situation is necessary for lifetime security, these are jobs your very special adult can do all his life. A busy life, feeling needed, is a happy life.

Our Downs Syndrome citizens have a happy way about them which stays with them always if they are treated fairly and with kindness.

16

The Preschool or Nursery Group

THE NURSERY SCHOOL PROGRAM is included in this book for two reasons: to help parents understand how a nursery school can help a child with retarded development to learn to listen and to learn to talk, and to help teachers directly.

Children grow as they learn to do things that have meaning and as they learn to control themselves so they can do these things for a purpose.

A child must pay attention and listen if he is to learn from what he is told. A child must pay attention to what he sees and touches, or he cannot learn from seeing and touching. He must store up experiences if he is to collect any ideas from his experiences. This storing-up of experiences and ideas is what *learning* really is.

A nursery school can help to guide the child through necessary experiences.

It is suggested by some people that the nursery-school-age child with delayed development be placed in a regular nursery school with normal children, the reason given for this being that the handicapped child will pick up ideas and language from his classmates and will imitate them.

This is urged strongly, by some schools of thought, for Downs Syndrome three-year-olds. In some cases this has been a successful course to follow, yet we must remember that as children imitate other children, they imitate without much judgment and pick up some habits that we wish they had not been exposed to.

Also the Downs Syndrome little one has a strong tendency to stutter if pushed too hard. In trying to keep up with the faster-moving children in a nursery school, this happens frequently enough to indicate that such placement is not the wise choice.

Our little handicapped children need very carefully planned learning experiences, planned specially for them, and this requires a special nursery school.

Because listening and talking are social activities, children can sometimes be helped more easily to learn to talk in a group than when they work with only one person. Of course, there are some children who need to work alone with an adult, but even these will need some chance to be with other children very nearly like themselves.

Everything children do in a nursery class is a part of communication. Receiving ideas from others and giving ideas to others is communication.

The ability *to receive ideas* from others, to follow directions, to respect other children, to share and to take turns requires the ability to listen.

Parents are understandably very anxious for a handicapped child to learn to talk. This concern is particularly sharp if the child has reached the age of four years without learning to talk. It is very necessary, both to the child's welfare and to that of the parents, for them to understand that the child must be helped to learn to listen before he can be taught to speak. The parents' best course of action is to work with the nursery school teacher, following her directions at home, rather then to try to rush ahead and help the child to talk without professional guidance.

The nursery school teacher will have regularly scheduled meetings with the parents of the children enrolled to share information about their children. The teacher needs to know the parents and to gain their cooperation. Meetings with just the mothers are very important, just to talk, to share, and to become friends.

It is very helpful to young daddies to have meetings with the teacher and also with a male counselor *without* the teacher present. Too often fathers are left out of school contacts and need someone to talk to just as much, maybe even more, than the mothers do.

If you are a parent of a child newly enrolled in a special nursery school, be sure to ask about getting together with the other parents. If such meetings are not a part of the school program, ask the teacher to work with you to organize a parents' group and keep at it until such a group is put together. A good nursery school will have such a group or will welcome your help in getting one organized. These meetings should be very informal and relaxed and not just gripe sessions or fund-raising committees. The purpose is to share ideas, concerns, and to learn as much as possible about helping your child at home.

The whole nursery school program is planned to teach children to listen and respond in the proper way. The proper way, at the beginning, is by *doing*, instead of *saying*.

Toward the end of the nursery school term, the children should be using their voices with meaning and ready to start saying words.

The problem given here for nursery school will probably

take a full school year—from September to June. Some of the groups may require a longer time. In this period the children are learning to listen.

Once in a while a word will pop out.

If this happens, the child should be carried along to use words but also should continue with the listening program, following directions, learning to share, and taking turns in all activities.

As you study the sample of the daily program, you can see how important listening is to each task to be done during the day. To do her best, the teacher of the nursery school class needs the help of every parent to carry on at home with understanding and sincere co-operation in her efforts to help the child.

The Purpose of a Preschool Program

A preschool nursery school for children with retarded development provides a planned program to help them grow in necessary ways.

In a nursery school, the child is with other children, is free from trying to keep up with brothers, sisters, and neighbors who are apt to expect him to do things he is not able to do or is not ready to do.

The young child can learn to control himself and get along with other people in a nursery group before he has too many failures in keeping up with his playmates.

A competent teacher will try to find out how each child learns. This information will help in planning each step as the child moves along through the school program.

A teacher who knows the child, works with his parents, and makes a careful study of his gains or failures to gain, and keeps careful records can help to plan a happier future for both child and family.

The Place

A quiet room with soft-colored walls and furniture is the best place to have a nursery class. The furniture should be the right size for children. The table should be a round one of proper size for six or else six-sided, with a beige or gray formica top—and with no decorations whatsoever. The chairs should have a grip in the back so the children can carry them easily.

The room should have a low counter with a sink and running water.

The bathroom should be directly off the classroom if possible. It should have a junior-size toilet and low washbowl. It is a good idea to place the roll of toilet tissue out of the reach of the small children until they learn not to play with it. An extra smaller toilet seat should be attached to the same hinge on the back of the toilet seat. The toilet can then be used comfortably by more children. An extra potty chair should be available.

A potty chair is better than the regular toilet for very young children (three years or less). Toilet "education" is much easier if a comfortable potty chair is used.

Two rocking chairs will be very useful for the restless children.

Upon the wall, a peg board, painted to blend with the wall and provided with hooks and shelves, will be useful.

A pocket chart, such as is used in the primary grades, will come in handy. (See Appendix C.)

A good record player is needed, with FM radio if possible. The record player should have a top that can be fastened securely. A cassette tape recorder is very useful in addition to the record player. (See Appendix D for use of tapes and cassettes.)

Cupboards for coats, with bins above for hats, mittens, and extra clothing, is needed. This cupboard should have some sort of a door—possibly a folding one—to conceal the contents during lesson times.

Cupboards and drawers should be provided for all teaching supplies.

Toys and materials should be kept out of sight and brought out only when they are to be used.

The room should be as uncluttered as possible so all attention can be directed to each planned learning experience. The play housekeeping corner should be screened off.

During planned teaching time the windows should be covered with plain draperies so the children will not be drawn to looking outside instead of paying attention to planned tasks. During free play and exploring time, the draperies should be open. It is quite an exciting event when a fire truck passes by or some other unexpected event happens.

A long, sturdy bench should be placed under the windows. This is handy for climbing up to look out the window when the draperies are opened. It is a good place to sit while getting boots and outer clothing on or off. Rolling bins can be built to fit under the bench to hold blocks and push toys. These are handy for taking over to a corner for one child to work or play alone.

The Teacher

The teacher for the young nursery group must, like all

teachers, love little children. She must be strong physically, good-natured, have a good sense of humor, be charitable, willing to do more than her share and have a sense of dramatic acting. She must be tidy and wear pretty, soft colors. The teacher is the prime example for the social growth of each child.

A well-trained nursery school or kindergarten teacher can become an excellent teacher for the dependent little child if she is able to change herself from the play-leader kind of teaching used in normal kindergarten to a "friendly sergeant."

Teachers trained to work with deaf children or learning-disabled children have an excellent background for such a training program, for the problem of communicating is similar in both cases.

The Children

The children must be ready to work in a group. Five children to a teacher and adult helper should be the limit. Before a child is accepted by a nursery school, the following things are desirable:

1. A report from a physician stating that the child is developmentally retarded or severely learning disabled, giving cause if possible, and that he is in good health, free from communicable disease, and has had routine immunizations.

2. A report from a qualified psychologist that the child is functioning above the profoundly disabled level and/or shows signs of not succeeding readily in a normal preschool group. Do not try to work with a profoundly retarded child in a nursery group. These children need very special one-

to-one help. They can and do learn many things but require individual attention without the distraction of group activity. A three-year-old profoundly retarded child needs the individual help offered in an early intervention program for children under three. They move into the group when able to tolerate the activity.

3. A visit to the home to become acquainted with the parents and to see how the child acts in his familiar surroundings. From this visit, the teacher should learn something about how the child plays and how the parents feel about the fact that the child is handicapped. She must explain, and be as certain as possible that the parents understand, that the child is a special child and what the nursery school is trying to do.

4. The child should be trained for bowel control most of the time. The child who is not completely toilet trained should not be refused admission upon this ground only. Many children who are not completely toilet trained at this age need the nursery school to help them learn this control. The very fact that the parents have not been able to completely train the child shows the need for help from someone else. Usually the toilet training is completed within a very short time after admission into the nursery school program. See reference to Azrin and Foxx in Appendix H.

5. The child should be able to bear his own weight and walk with a minimum of help.

6. If the school serves the multiply handicapped, the child should be able to sit in a wheelchair, or walker, using whatever support is necessary. The Hoag chair, used for transporting some cerebral-palsied children, is not very comfortable for an entire session. A comfortable wheelchair should be used.

Why We Teach the Way We Do

It is very important to plan and to control every part of the program. *It must not be permissive.* This means the child must not be allowed always to choose what he wants to do, how he wants to do it, or when he wants to do it. This close planning is needed to give the child security, safety, and a chance to learn to pay attention. Some free playtime is part of the program, but most of the time is controlled very carefully.

1. *Security*

A window washer, working on an office building, uses a safety belt. This is his security. If he fastens this safety belt properly, he can lean back on it and pay attention to his work. He knows just how far it will let him lean back. Children need to know just how far they can go. This is their security.

Knowing what to expect next by following a daily routine and having no doubts about what is good and what is not good helps a young handicapped child to feel secure. This security is satisfying to all children during their early years. Learning to adjust to breaks in routine can come later. Bringing a little handicapped child to a strange place, to new grown-ups, teachers, etc., to new demands and rules, is a big step away from the familiar surroundings of home. As early as possible in this new "away from home" business, a child should gain a feeling that things are stable and dependable. A child may look forward to music time and its relaxation. He will behave through a harder lesson because he looks forward to music time. If music time doesn't come when he expects it he is very likely to act up, because he can't understand disappointment.

Rules must be set and not changed until the child is old enough to know why they have been changed. If one cupboard or drawer is off limits and used as an example in learning "don't touch," it must stay that way for a long period of time. Similarly, the cupboard and bins that are to be used by the children freely or by direction must not suddenly be off limits. It's hard enough for a child to know what grown-ups mean without having the rules suddenly changed. When a set of rules is learned the child can relax and put his attention on a new task.

2. *Safety*

A planned and guided program for special children helps to avoid dangers in play situations. It is a safety measure. For instance, a sandbox is a wonderful place to play, a place to experiment with the sense of feeling, to see how sand moves through your fingers, how cold or how warm it is, how damp it is. You can do so much with sand . . . but *it is not for throwing*. A handful of sand in the face can create a fear that might take weeks to overcome. Sandbox play must be properly guided to be useful.

Early training in the meaning of "no," "come to me," "don't touch," "sit down" is a *must* for safety and for getting along in a group.

3. *Learning to pay attention*

Directing effort, or learning to pay attention to doing a certain task, is very hard for all children. They must be helped to learn how to pay attention and taught to look directly at your eyes when you are telling them something, such as giving a direction. They are all easily distracted and have a very hard time staying interested in one thing for any length of time.

Fascinating gadgets, such as wind-ups, monkeys that shake a bell or beat on a drum, are excellent attention getters. Such attention getters also help to learn about "don't touch," and "O.K.—you may touch—but gently." A lucite hourglass is a fascinating toy.

To get a child's attention and hold it, you must be a real ham actor and use some very attention-compelling things; use sounds he has heard, words he can understand, things that he has seen or touched or smelled or tasted. You must give him things to handle that he is able to hold.

When you have gained his attention, you can add new ideas; but he must be captured with something he already knows about or that fascinates him. (This does not include things like a pacifier or a "security blanket.")

It is always tempting to give a very cute or pretty toy to a child or to urge him to look at a picture book even if he is not ready for it. If he pushes the toy or book away, or tries to smash or tear it, you will know that he is not ready for it.

A child learns about his world by tasting, touching, patting, squeezing, squashing, lifting, dropping, splashing, throwing, pushing, pulling, and all sorts of combinations of these actions. The child with retarded development may not do all these things and needs to be helped and guided through this necessary learning time.

A child can hardly be expected to stack the tree blocks if he has not yet learned how to pick up a block on purpose and to put it down on purpose.

He needs many opportunities to be busy in directed play with sand, clay, water, cotton balls to pick up and squeeze, big balls to push and chase or to pick up and drop, big blocks to shove around or to pick up and to put down (gently).

He is interested in himself and what affects him. He would rather hear about himself, play by himself, and control everything, including the teacher, just for himself.

The child with retarded development stays in this "self" stage much longer than the normal child and people may say he is spoiled and pampered. Like all children, he must live through this phase but he needs help to move him along to be interested in other people and what they do, and to respect their rights, to share time, attention, and treasures.

The teacher can and should use this interest in self to gain the child's attention. The child's own name is used rather than pronouns. He must not be expected to play and share with another child until he has learned to play by himself without bothering other children and has learned that this is a good idea.

Learning to play alone, without grabbing or bumping (this is called parallel play), requires close watching. Keeping the nursery group small, with one adult for two children, will allow this careful watching and help the child learn this very important lesson.

"Learning to listen" goes on *all* the time the child is in the nursery group. He is also learning to follow directions.

Learning to listen in a group situation is different from learning to listen with an adult whose attention is devoted solely to the one child. In a group, sharing starts immediately. Taking turns is the order of the day and for the handicapped child who has received practically all the grownups' attention at home, this is a difficult challenge.

Guidance and planning must be carefully done, but the teacher *must not* become harsh or severe. For example, "no" must have meaning but the child must be shown immediately afterward that he is loved. It is what *he did* that is not loved. He needs a smile and love so that he can be sure the teacher really knows he is going to be good.

To learn about the world around him a child must experience many things that will have meaning to him. To explore toys, the rooms of his home, his schoolroom, it is necessary to touch and move things. Children with retarded development often are slow and clumsy in using their hands. Hands and eyes must work together, so let's study how this develops.

How Children Grow in Using Hands and Eyes
Level I

Use of hands.

    A Reach for something with whole hand spread out flat. A baby will reach and cover what he is after and clutch it in the palm of the hand. Usually what he picks up will be brought to his mouth with the object showing on the little-finger side of the hand, as a dagger would be held. His eyes see what he is reaching for but will not usually follow his hand as the object is moved toward his mouth. He will let go of the object just by straightening out his fingers. The thumb is not used at this level.

    B Reach for something with both arms: a soft ball, easy-to-grab squishy stuffed toy. He will just drop the object when no longer interested. Eyes will look at what he picks up.

    C Hold something large that is placed in his arms like a stuffed animal, a big doll, a large, soft ball. He will drop the object very soon. His eyes seldom look at what he is holding. It wasn't his idea to pick it up in the first place. He is still using a flat hand grasp at this stage. Thumbs are not used at this time.

    D Now as he learns to pull things to him by curling his fingers and using his full hand, *except* his thumb, he will bring things to his mouth with the object showing at the thumb-side of his hand. He has learned to bend his elbow slightly and to twist his wrist just enough to get things to his mouth in a shovel, or scoop type of motion. The thumb may or may not be used. Now his eyes can follow the object until it is quite close to his mouth. It looks like he is holding a thing in his fist. Until a child can use his hands this way, like a shovel or scoop, he cannot be expected to eat with a spoon, pull a zipper, or handle buttons.

Although a child can manage to start using a spoon, he must not be expected to do things that require use and control of the thumb until he is ready.

At this stage, the very young child will first play with things without using his eyes for guidance or with very little eye contact, except possibly locating what he wants. Many little ones will be surrounded by toys, too many toys, and will just accidently grab something without looking. He seems to be *feeling* and listening to the sounds around him. Good toys at this point are things to hear, like rattles, musical blocks, squeaking soft toys.

The child with retarded development will need more experience to help him along. He is no longer a baby in size but may be using his eyes and hands like a baby.

Use sand, water, things to squeeze like clay or sponges, both dry and wet.

Give him things to handle like cotton balls, pieces of cotton cloth, a woolen mitten, a leather mitten, a spoon. Children need many experiences handling a big variety of things. As you play along touching and stroking and squeezing these various textures, talk (very briefly) about what you are feeling. "Soft," "smooth," "um-nice," "rough," "sticky," "hard," "slippery," "wet," "dry." Dream up many things to touch and talk about. Be sure it's fun for both of you.

To review how a child grows in using hands and eyes, here is a list that tells you how a baby will usually progress.

A Clutches his fist and holds anything put in his hand very tensely during the first six or eight weeks of his life. He does not control the clutch or the release of what he is holding. This is called a *reflex* action, just touching the palm of the hand will cause the fingers to bend. When this type of grasp continues long after eight weeks, it is a sign of slowed down neurological development. (Such a neurological development can be detected also when the baby's cry sounds don't change from the wail of the newborn to crying in different pitch and melody. Crying sounds should change at about six to eight weeks.)

B Watches own hands while lying on back.

C Touches, scratches at sheets, bumpers in crib.

D Plays with fingers as both hands meet.

E Grasps for something, whole hand closing on object, palm of hand touching first. This is called the *palmar grasp*.

F Squeezes and releases squeaky soft toys. Child may pick up toy himself, if he touches it, or just hold onto what is put into his hands.

G Brings objects to mouth: the little-finger side of hand gets to the mouth first, rattle held like a *dagger*. This is called a *dagger grasp*.

H Slaps, pushes against toys: slaps and splashes water; hand is quite flat, palm touching first.

I Reaches and explores by touching or pushing.

J Grasps and shakes a rattle.

K Holds large toy with both hands.

L About this time the baby will start to shift his grasp to the thumb side of his hand, yet he will not use his thumb very much to help manage a steady hold. This is called a *scoop or shovel grasp*. He should be able to start using a spoon for eating. *Eyes are now directing his hands.*

M Reaches, grasps, holds, and voluntarily lets go.

N Grasps and transfers toys from one hand to another.

O Plays patty-cake with help.

P Reaches with some definite plan of direction.

Q Pokes with forefinger.

R Claps hands, holding fingers spread out.

S Holds a beaded peg, crayon, or pencil in a *scissors grasp*: thumb pushing against the middle of the first finger.

T Picks up and holds smaller object with a *pincer grasp*: thumb tip and first finger tip pushing against each other.

U Holds something with one hand and does something to it with other hand, such as steadying the hammer bench with one hand, or steadying the peg while using the hammer with other hand.

V Picks up something and puts it somewhere on purpose; puts blocks or balls into a container; fills a peg board.
(Start with large-head topped pegs.)
Just filling the peg board is all we want at first. Copying patterns, sorting, making straight lines on a peg board will come a little later.

Level II

Noticing that things are different or alike because of size, shape, color, or texture. (Review Chapter 10.)

A Baby handles smaller things than in Level I; uses smaller head pegs, progressing to plain pegs without bead top: smaller blocks: parquetry blocks.

B Places things in right order, nesting blocks or cylinders, lines up various sized blocks according to size from big to little or from little to big. The whole idea of putting things in *order* is very important in the entire learning process. Eyes must guide hands to do this.

Level III

Putting parts together to make something whole.
This means the eyes must make the connection and guide the hands. Noticing that things are different or alike, what is seen and touched now means something very, very

special; the child can put parts that have meaning (that he knows about) together in combinations and constructions to make a different and another whole object.

A Arranges blocks to make a bridge or a house.

B Strings beads in a pattern.

C Uses crayons and paper; paintbrushes and paper; paste and paper; scissors, paste, and paper. Be sure he is using a scissors grasp.

D Pushes a button: winds things up or pushes a lever to make something move or do something special.

Level IV

Using all these skills under direction to learn how to do something else.

This is called "carryover." This level is not reached very often until the child has progressed through the nursery school program. Children will, however, learn to pass things, such as paper napkins, and set plates and spoons on place mats.

Many children with retarded development will continue to hold things like a dagger for a long time. They will hold a large crayon like a dagger to scribble. When a child is in this stage of the development of the grasp function—and many five- and six-year-olds still hold things like this—do not expect him to use a spoon for feeding, to unbutton or to button, pull a zipper, and surely not to use a pair of scissors.

Many children with retarded development will use a dagger grasp long after they are *able* to use a shovel or scoop grasp, a scissors grasp, or pincer grasp. It is a matter of habit and need for motivation.

It is quite easy to find out if the child *can* use a better grasp or really is not yet *able* to do it. Put some sugar cereal bits, or bits of cookie, in front of him. If he picks up the food, using his thumb and first finger, he *can* use a better grasp and just needs to be urged and helped to want to do it.

One way to help him use a better grasp when you are certain he *can* do it is to not use big jumbo crayons. Use short, little, thin crayon pieces, not more than two inches long. He cannot hold the little piece of crayon like a dagger, and if he wants to use the crayon, he must use his thumb and first finger. Also do not use the large 1-inch-diameter dowels in form boards. Use the jumbo-headed pegs and boards. See page 218, Ideal School Supply.

If the child *cannot* pick up the food bits using his thumb, he needs help to move from using the dagger grasp to using the shovel, scissors, and pincer grasps. Then it is necessary for you to provide a lot of exciting activities to help him to improve his grasp skill. Squeezing sponges in water, squeezing a medicine dropper full of bright-colored vegetable dye into a white container holding clear water are real fascinators. It's fun to pop the bubbles on plastic packing materials used to protect fragile things for shipping.

Put your hand over the child's hand to help him get the feeling of using his hand in a better grasp. Help him, reward him, praise him, and have fun yourself with these games.

Here is a great big reminder. *PLEASE DO NOT TRY TO TEACH A CHILD TO USE SCISSORS UNTIL YOU ARE VERY SURE HE CAN USE A SCISSORS GRASP.* That thumb must be actively useful and controlled before scissors can be managed.

Management of clothing depends upon grasp development. A child can push down pants without much help of the thumb, but it's rather hard to pull them up. A scissors grasp is essential to unbuttoning, buttoning, snapping, or zipping and most clothing management.

If the child cannot, or does not, comfortably move from the dagger grasp, wait, help him to get those little hands ready by making just one move ahead at a time. He must progress through the shovel grasp, to the scissors grasp, and then to the pincer grasp. If you move slowly, using many fun experiences, it will be easy and a happy rewarding experience for both you and the child.

How Children Grow in Experience

Level I

They are interested only in themselves.

Level II

They become interested in things and using them. They also can learn that another child may use something that belongs just to that other child. But children at this level of social growth are not yet ready to share and take turns.

Level III

They become interested in people, who they are, what they do, and how they affect each other. Now sharing is possible and necessary.

Sample of Action During Roll Call

The class is seated around a table, an adult between each two children. The teacher has a book for recording attendance, preferably a bright-colored one. A little overflourishing of the pencil helps keep eyes directed toward the teacher.

She says, "Let's see—who is here?"

She calls the name "Tommy," actually singing it, and says, "Is Tommy here?" not looking at Tommy immediately. Give Tommy time to try to get *you* to look at *him*. Be surprised when you pretend you just realized he is present.

Tommy will probably smile. The teacher says, "Yes," nodding her head, "Tommy is here," and records it in her book, repeating "Tommy is here" and smiling.

If Tommy is absent, she says, "Tommy isn't here—too bad," and shakes her head, looking very sad.

If Tommy is present but does not respond, the teacher reaches toward him with the palm of her hand upward. If Tommy does not touch her hand, she gently places his hand in hers and smiles.

After a few trials, Tommy will be willing to touch the teacher's hand and smile.

Whether your handicapped child attends an early intervention program, a nursery school, or you teach him yourself, you as a parent will be the major teacher because you have many more hours with him each day. Don't be afraid to work with your child. The school needs you very much, and with some study, practice, and confidence on your part, you can help your child communicate.

Curriculum for Young Children with Retarded Development

WHAT YOU WANT THE CHILD TO DO	HOW YOU DO IT	WHAT YOU USE
	Nursery I *Beginners—first group experience.*	
PHYSICAL GROWTH		
Self-help		
Remove outer clothing.	With help. Use Behavior Shaping Techniques.	Child's own coat.
Learn about wet and dry.	A doll that "wets" after being "fed" a bottle is a very good teaching device. Have the child feed the doll—the doll has *dry* pants on—and watch the pants get wet. The child hears you say, "Oh! Your baby has *wet* pants. Let's change them for	A doll that "wets" after being "fed."

WHAT YOU WANT THE CHILD TO DO	HOW YOU DO IT	WHAT YOU USE
	nice *dry* pants." After a few practice sessions with the doll, have your child put the doll on the potty chair just as soon as the doll has been "fed." Praise the doll for urinating in the potty. Now let the child *teach* the doll to use the potty to "wet" (or whatever word you have decided to use). Praise the doll! It should be quite easy to shift the idea from the doll's performance to the child's performance. Be sure you give the child your *full*	

Stay dry.	warm attention and much, much praise and reward. (See reference to Arzin & Foxx, page 220.) Use two pairs of training pants. Dampen one pair. Have child handle the pants as you say, "Dry—nice"— "wet" and look sad. Take to toilet periodically.	Two pairs of training pants. Toilet seat must be proper size and comfortable. If child is afraid of toilet, use a potty chair. Always use a potty chair for very small children.
Help with clothes in bath-room.	By the time the child is staying dry, he should require a minimum of help.	

WHAT YOU WANT THE CHILD TO DO	HOW YOU DO IT	WHAT YOU USE
EMOTIONAL GROWTH		
Know hands must be washed after going to the toilet.	Requires help. Not yet ready to mix hot and cold or to rinse and dry thoroughly.	Washbowl should be low enough to use comfortably.
Eat food without help—not requiring a spoon. Handle drinking cup or glass.	Requires help. Present very small amount at one time.	Cookie or sandwich, cut in small pieces. Milk cup, not too big. Use plastic cup or plastic drinking glass.
Engage in large-muscle activity.	Carefully supervise *all* activity. Do not turn the group loose with many things—two things at one time are plenty to choose from.	8-inch rough-finish rubber balls. Playground barrels. Large toys to push. Floormat to roll around on (gym mat).

	Cart to pull, preferably a bin on wheels.
	Doll buggy to push.
	Rolling toys to ride on and push along with feet (no pedals at this time).
	Large blocks to carry.
	Large boxes to crawl in and out of.
	Rocking horse.
	Rocking boat.
	Sandbox (covered—when not in use).
	Pots and pans and large spoons for sandbox.
	Swinging gate.
	A place to sit away from the group.
Show self-control; learn not to bite, hit, or push.	Remove from group immediately, and say, "No. Not funny."

184

WHAT YOU WANT THE CHILD TO DO	HOW YOU DO IT	WHAT YOU USE
Engage in parallel play.	Teacher selects an activity for each child in a different part of the room or playground. Watch closely.	Sandbox; large-muscle activity materials, such as barrels, swinging gate, large balls.

SOCIAL GROWTH

WHAT YOU WANT THE CHILD TO DO	HOW YOU DO IT	WHAT YOU USE
Listen and respond to "No," "Come to me," "Don't touch," "Sit down."	See Chapter 8. Use child's name at beginning of each direction given. ("Mary, come to me.")	See Chapter 8.
Listen and accept approval, "Yes" (with nod of head from teacher); also "Good boy" or "Good girl."		
Understand "yours," "mine."	This will not be learned for the first few months. It is	

		taught the same way "no" is taught.	Use words "yours" and "mine."

Learn to use one toy at a time.

Careful planning and selecting interesting and loved toys. Sit at the table, each child with his own toy. Help child keep his interest upon own toy. Do not allow grabbing or snatching.

During music time, wait turn to use favorite instrument. Take turns being "first" in being served, helped, or in selecting a toy. Take turns on playground equipment.

Begin to take turns and share.

Be fair with all the children and do not allow any child to take a turn or toy that belongs to someone else.

Use Behavior Modification Techniques.

Carry out one simple direction such as "Give it to me, please."

WHAT YOU WANT THE CHILD TO DO	HOW YOU DO IT	WHAT YOU USE
INTELLECTUAL GROWTH		
Recognize own wraps, mittens, etc. Recognize place for own wraps.	With help—should learn this quickly.	Wardrobe and bin of proper size marked with child's first name on a colored card.
Handle materials (purposefully, without throwing).	Constant control.	
Level I *Just handle and explore things.*		
Learn basic motor skills through structured programming.	A Reach for something, usually with whole hand. Let go of something. Grasp something like holding a dagger.	Sand. Water. Clay. Fabrics.

B Use thumb against first finger to hold, feel, or manipulate something.	Fleece. Sponge. Large balls.
1 *Without using eyes* child is feeling or listening as you say appropriate word or words. Use sand, damp and dry; water, warm and cold; things to squeeze like clay, sponges; things to handle like cotton, wool, velvet, corduroy, rough and smooth shapes (see page 99); things to hear like rattles, musical blocks, jingle bells, speaking toys.	Large blocks. Rattle. Bells. Musical blocks. Humming tops. Soft toys easy to pick up. Large push toys. Peg boards—1-inch dowel. Peg boards — jumbo-headed pegs. Spoons. Pictures that squeak like the animals they show. Spread out clay to poke holes in. If you make cookies in school, let each child poke a little spot to hold colored sugar.

WHAT YOU WANT THE CHILD TO DO	HOW TO DO IT	WHAT YOU USE
	2 Using eyes Use things to push—large wooden cars, trucks, etc.; pictures that squeak when squeezed.	Small containers. Plastic color chips.
	C Both arms reach for something.	
	D Both arms hold something large like stuffed animals or a big doll. (It's no wonder Raggedy Ann is so beloved—she is so easy to pick up and so beautiful!)	
	E Use fingers to poke at something.	

F One hand holds something and other hand does something.

G Hands pick up something and place it someplace on purpose; put balls or blocks in containers; place 1-inch dowels in form boards or jumbo-headed pegs in peg board.

Constant control. Be sure there is nothing around the room to bother or distract the children. Their attention must be saved for the learning task in front of them. Keep a portable screen around the "housekeeping" corner.

Direct attention to adult.

WHAT YOU WANT THE CHILD TO DO	HOW TO DO IT	WHAT YOU USE

Nursery II *Graduates of Beginners Group—six children can be managed in this group with two adults. (This group must have had group experience and have learned the tasks of beginners group.)*

PHYSICAL GROWTH

Self-care

WHAT YOU WANT THE CHILD TO DO	HOW TO DO IT	WHAT YOU USE
Care for outer wraps with very little help. Should put outer wraps on with some help.	Behavior Shaping Techniques.	
Go to bathroom routinely or without being reminded, care for self at toilet with very little help.		
Wash hands after toileting with very little help or reminding.		
Handle spoon and drink	Help by steering and balanc-	Start with easy - to - handle

from cup or glass without spilling.	ing—also show the child how.	foods, such as ice cream in Dixie cups (Jell-O is *hard* to handle).
Continue large-muscle activity.	Start to use smaller balls and blocks as child learns to handle large things easily.	
Begin to use smaller materials.	Guide child's hands.	½-inch dowel—peg board—beaded large pegs (Ideal) small crayons (short pieces). ¾-inch paintbrushes. Hammering blocks.
EMOTIONAL GROWTH *Self-control* Follow through on tasks of own choice.	Child must complete one before trying the next. Always insist materials be put in proper place before next thing is selected.	
Accept changes in routine.	Occasionally change routine and make it fun. If routine must be changed, teacher	

WHAT YOU WANT THE CHILD TO DO	HOW TO DO IT	WHAT YOU USE
	must not act upset. She can use this to help the children learn about changes.	
SOCIAL GROWTH		
Listen and respond appropriately (still not trying to say real words).	Responds to own name in roll call by smiling, shaking hands, or raising hand.	
	Circle activity.	Name cards in color. Progress to name cards without color cues.
Identify familiar things by hearing them named.	Respond appropriately (in this progression) to "Show me," "Bring me," "Give me."	Use common objects within experience of child. See Appendix word list.
Start and stop activity on command or cues.	Children in row of chairs far enough apart not to be able to touch each other.	Clapping hands. Rhythm sticks with recorded music.

Vocalize.	Humming, vocalizing, imitating animal and familiar sounds.	
Progress in verbalization.	See Chapter 9.	
Use proper words for parts of body—going to the toilet.	Insist upon proper words.	Insistence and parent cooperation.
Take turns.	Consistent management.	
Begin to play together.	Share an activity. Share sandbox space and toys. Exchange toys.	Rolling or tossing large ball. Pulling each other in rolling bin. Sandbox. Sandbox toys.
Work hard on following directions.	Give commands carefully and clearly.	When you are very sure you have child's attention, and eye contact, give commands such as "Put the baby in the buggy and the book on the table." Child should pro-

WHAT YOU WANT THE CHILD TO DO	HOW TO DO IT	WHAT YOU USE
		gress to following three commands.
Go to and from transportation unescorted.	Careful watching.	
Show respect for adults and peers.	Careful watching.	
Show good manners with visitors.	Careful watching.	
INTELLECTUAL GROWTH		
Learn parts of body. (See body awareness section in Performance Goal Record, *Trainable Children*, page 220 below.)	Group activity.	Use records, such as "I Wash My Doll," "Put Your Finger in the Air." See page 224 for more titles. Assemble doll puzzles (puzzle plaque—5 pieces).
Show respect for others:	Take own chair to proper	

Remain quiet. Step aside.	place in circle or return chair to former place without bumping or pushing. Learn what "sh" means.	Big chair and little chair. Big doll and little doll. Big bottle and little bottle. Big and little balls, cubes. (See page 93). Stacking trees.
Increase attention span.	Longer circle activity period—carefully planned.	
Level II *Noticing things are different or alike because of size, then by shape, then by color.*	A Handle smaller things. Use jumbo-headed pegs and progress to smaller pegs and boards.	Nesting blocks. 1-inch—assorted colors—*not decorated.*
Begin learning to handle materials for a definite reason; now eyes help hands.	B Place things in right order. Copy a simple pattern on a peg board.	

WHAT YOU WANT THE CHILD TO DO	HOW TO DO IT	WHAT YOU USE
	1 Match and sort by size. 2 Match and sort by shape. 3 Match and sort by color. 4 By size, shape, and color, select *red circles*, *blue stars*, etc.	Common objects in assorted sizes and colors, such as small toy cars, plastic spoons. 1-inch cubes in assorted colors (see page 204). Jumbo peg boards.
Respond to slow, fast, funny, not funny, happy, sad.	Walk, run, to selected music or tom-tom. In sharing activities.	Small peg boards. Form boards. Mosaic boards. Colored wooden circles, squares, triangles, diamonds, stars. (Have enough to allow each child to have 3 or 4 of each item for identifying and sorting.) Use only primary colors.

		Use funny to share a laugh; "not funny" for unacceptable behavior, if child laughs about it.
		Apply proper word and facial expression during roll call: "Tom is here. We are *happy*"; "Tom is not *here*. Tom is sick—sad."
		Use "happy" for good deeds and "sad" for scolds.
		Present pictures (a child smiling; a child crying or frowning).
Recognize own name and names of others in the group.	Select printed names without color cues from pocket chart or recognize own things.	Use name cards in pocket chart.
		Use children's own things.
		Present a coat or cap to group, child selects correct owner and/or places it in proper bin.
Graduate from the need of	Use true pictures.	This is a long and hard task.

WHAT YOU WANT THE CHILD TO DO	HOW TO DO IT	WHAT YOU USE
objects to pictures with tactile, textured surfaces to flat pictures as such progress is indicated.	See Chapter 9.	See Chapter 9.
Learn about foods that are good for us.	Circle time.	Pictures of milk, apples, meat, chicken. See page 205 for list.
Learn about warm and cold.	Talk about weather *very* briefly.	Feel water, heat vents, glass, etc.
	Talk about cold and warm days.	
	Touch "warm" and "cold" things.	
Learn more about wet and dry.	Talk about rainy and sunshiny days.	Use sponges, Kleenex.

17

Dos and Don'ts

Do PLAN your lessons.

DON'T work too long.

DO use a mirror if attention is hard to hold; this is very helpful with tongue and lip exercises.

DO name things—name each piece of clothing while dressing or undressing. Name foods served, etc.

DO count—every chance that comes along. Young retarded children will parrot or mimic the sound of counting. The numbers do not actually mean anything to them until they are trained to have some concepts of what numbers mean. This rote counting (as the parroted counting is called) will be helpful later on. Count things whenever you can, in a sort of singsong way. For example, when picking up his shoe and his socks, say, "One-two—two shoes." Count the chairs as you place them around the table. Count the spoons as you put them down.

DON'T send your child to the store until he is ready to make such a trip alone. There is always some unkind or unknowing person who could make your child feel very sad. Be sure he can say what he wants or can safely deliver a note to the storekeeper.

DO hum and sing around the house. It will be good for your child and also help you to relax. You can't sing and gripe at the same time.

DO learn to finger-paint and have fun sloshing paint around with your child. Clean up together!

DON'T interrupt your child if you don't want him to interrupt you.

DO give your child time to answer a remark addressed to him.

DON'T always answer for him.

DO remember that stories must be real. A child will listen better if you make up stories about *him*, favorite toys, playmates, and members of the family.

DO select very short stories. Use your child's name in place of the name used in the book whenever you can.

DO read Mother Goose rhymes and jingles. Read the familiar ones over and over again. You may be bored, but your child isn't. Be a real "ham." When your child has started to say words, read favorite poems and leave out the last word (keeping your voice up) so he can say that last word. For example: "Little Bo" (stop)—child says "Peep"; "Has lost her" (stop)—child says "sheep"; etc. The words may not be too good but it's fun and your child will be delighted.

DO play with hand puppets. Use two puppets. Start out just having your puppet bow, and have the child's puppet do the same thing. You can do all sorts of things with a pair of puppets and have a good time doing them.

DO have a variety of material to use. Keep adding more gimmicks. *You* can get bored with too much of the same thing, just as your child can get bored.

Do have fun and let your child know you really are having fun.

DO remember rewards are food, then hugs, smiles, words, and always *Love*.

Appendix on Materials

A   Materials You Will Need

Small basket or box about the size of a shoe box.
Red rubber ball about 5 inches in diameter.
Red rubber ball about 3 inches in diameter (a red tennis ball
   would do).
Yellow rubber ball about 5 inches in diameter.
Yellow rubber ball about 3 inches in diameter.
Toy boat—a safe one to play with in the bathtub.
Bell—a dinner bell or a plastic one from a set of bells about 3
   inches tall.
Small baby doll about 8 inches long.
Toy bus about 5 inches long that looks like a real bus.
Toy bus about 2 or 3 inches long.
Toy bunny rabbit about 8 inches long.
Toy bird—there is a very good metal bird that winds up and
   cheeps.
Dollhouse bed.
Dollhouse bathroom set, toilet, washbowl, and bathtub.
(You will need a whole set of dollhouse furniture later. You
   need just the bed and bathroom set at first.)

2 sets of jingle bells. ⎫ You can buy these at a
2 maracas or dried gourds that rattle. ⎬ large music store or
2 rhythm sticks. ⎭ make them yourself.

Soft feather about 5 or 6 inches long with a piece of yarn about 10 inches long tied to it.

A mirror at least 4 inches by 6 inches.

Box of clear plastic straws.

Some very small lollipops.

Candle in tip-proof holder.

2 cardboard rolls from toilet tissue.

2 cardboard rolls from paper towels.

2 fat (milkshake) sipper straws.

1 box Milton Bradley 1-inch cubes, mixed colors—order from a school supply company (see classified telephone directory).

Noisemakers that moo, meow, or make any animal sounds. These are little cylinders with pictures on them.

Peg boards—available where educational toys are sold (Ideal School Supply).

An easel or a pocket chart—you can make your own easel (see instructions on page 215).

FOR MAKING YOUR SET OF PICTURES

9-inch x 12-inch tag board—a package of 100 sheets is the best way to buy it from a stationery store.

9-inch x 12-inch construction paper—one package of mixed colors.

Bottle of rubber cement or Elmer's Glue.

B Pictures You Will Need

You won't find all these pictures at once. You don't need them all at once, but you should keep your eyes open for good pictures you can use later. Use colored pictures. You can find many very good pictures in magazines and old calendars. Cut away most of the background, being sure to leave *no* printing. You don't need to "paper doll" cut, but be sure you don't have anything but the picture of the object or action you want. These words are listed alphabetically—*not* in order of difficulty—or sequence of development.

1. *Pictures for b, p, m words.* This is the starter word list.

	b		p	*m*
baby	bed	bread	pen	mama (use a
bacon	bell	bug	pencil	snapshot)
ball	bike	bunny	pickle	man
banana	boat	bus	pipe	meat
bathroom	bottle	butter	pop	milk
bathtub	box	bye-bye	potty	money
beach	boy		puppy	moon

Pictures of familiar things. This is a basic vocabulary for language training. These are words for which pictures can be found as well as a basic vocabulary for all preschool children.

HOME AND RELATED ITEMS

Furniture

bed	lamp	stool
chair	picture	stove
clock	radio	table
dresser	rug	telephone
fan	sewing machine	television (TV)
ironing board	sink	wastebasket

Desk Items

book	package	ruler
calendar	paper	scissors
crayons	paste	shelf
desk	pen	stamp
envelope	pencil	typewriter
letter	pin	

Rooms

bathroom	den	laundry
bedroom	dining room	living room
closet	kitchen	recreation room

Personal Items

bracelet	lipstick	ring
comb	necklace	toothbrush
earring	perfume	toothpaste
hairbrush	powder	watch
Kleenex	razor	

Tools

hammer	rake	screwdriver
nail	sandpaper	shovel
pliers	saw	

Musical Instruments

bell	guitar	organ
drum	horn	piano

Clothing

apron	hat	shirt
bathrobe	jacket	shoes
belt	jeans	shorts
blouse	mittens	skirt
boots	nightgown	snowsuit
button	pajamas	socks
cap	pants	suit
coat	pocketbook	sweater
dress	purse	swimsuit
glove	raincoat	tie
handkerchief	scarf	zipper

Household

banister	floor	porch
blanket	garbage	roof
broom	gate	soap
bucket	key	stairs
can	home	towel
chimney	house	wall
door	lamp	washcloth
fence	light	window
fireplace	mop	yard

Transportation

airplane	car	train
bicycle	fire engine	tricycle
bus	motorcycle	truck

Materials

board	cotton	rubber
cardboard	glass	steel
clay	leather	wood
cloth	paper	wool

Money

dime	fifty cents	penny
dollar	nickel	quarter

Colors

black	green	purple
blue	orange	red
brown	pink	yellow

Numbers

one	five	nine
two	six	ten
three	seven	
four	eight	

Miscellaneous

chalk	movie	story
circus	music	string
flag	party	sun
hole	rock	wheel
map	star	wind
moon	stick	

FOOD AND RELATED ITEMS

MEATS	VEGETABLES	FRUITS
bacon	beans	apple
cheese	carrot	banana
chicken	celery	cherry
egg	corn	grape
fish	lettuce	grapefruit
ham	peas	orange
hamburger	potato	peach
hot dog	pumpkin	pear
roast	radish	pineapple
steak	squash	plum
turkey	tomato	strawberry

Sports Equipment

baseball	golf club	sled
baseball bat	hockey stick	slide
baseball glove	ice skate	swing
basketball	jungle gym	tennis ball
football	roller skate	tennis racket

Toys

ball	doll buggy	marble
balloon	dollhouse	puzzle
blocks	drum	sand
box	gun	scooter
cards	horn	top
doll	jumping rope	wagon
doll bed	kite	whistle

Verbs

bark	dress	lick
been	drink	lift
bite	drive	like
blow	drop	listen
bounce	eat	look
break	excuse (me)	made
bring	fall	may
brush	feed	measure
build	fill	melt
burn	find	move
button	finish	open
buy	fly	paint
call	fold	paste
can	found	pet
carry	get	pin
catch	give	pinch
chase	go	play
clap	had	pour
clean	hang	print
climb	have	pull
close	hear	push
comb	help	put
come	hide	race
cook	hit	rake
cough	hold	read
count	hunt	rest
cover	hurt	ride
crawl	iron	roll
cry	is	rub
cut	isn't	run
dance	jump	sail
did	keep	saw
dig	kick	scratch
do	kiss	scrub
draw	know	see
dream	laugh	sew

shake	stay	wait
shine	surprise	walk
shovel	sweep	want
show	swim	was
shut	swing	wash
sing	take	wave
sit	talk	wear
skate	tear	weight
slap	thank	were
sleep	think	wet
slide	throw	whip
smell	tie	will
smile	told	wipe
sneeze	took	won't
spank	touch	work
spend	turn	wrap
spill	unbutton	write
splash	undress	yawn
stand	use	

Contrast Words

all—one	dry—wet	loud—soft
any—some	fast—slow	more—less
awake—asleep	fat—thin	neat—messy
bad—good	first—last	new—old
before—after	full—empty	noisy—quiet
big—little	happy—sad	rough—smooth
broken—fixed	hard—soft	round—square
clean—dirty	heavy—light	sharp—dull
cold—hot	hungry—full	sick—well
curly—straight	large—small	
different—same	long—short	

Pronouns

he	him	I
her	his	it

me	that	what
mine	them	who
my	they	whose
our	this	you
she	we	your(s)

Prepositions

about	for	to
as	in	with
at	into	
before	on	

Drinks

chocolate milk	lemonade	tea
coffee	milk	water
Coke	juice	
Kool-Aid	pop	

Eating Utensils

bowl	glass	plate
cup	knife	spoon
dish	napkin	tray
fork	pan	

Treats

bread	ice cream	popcorn
butter	Jell-O	potato chip
cake	jelly	pretzel
candy	pancakes	pudding
cookie	peanut butter	sandwich
cracker	pickle	
doughnut	pie	

LOCATIONS AND CONDITIONS

Town

barber shop	church	drug store
bowling alley	downtown	fire station

garage	movie theater	shoe store
grocery store	park	sidewalk
home	post office	store
hospital	restaurant	street
house	school	zoo

Country

barn	highway	pasture
farm	hill	woods
field	meadow	

Seasons

spring	summer	fall	winter

Directions

front	start	under
back	stop	over
right	top	up
left	bottom	down
beside		

Weather Conditions

cloud(y)	ice	snow
cold	lightning	sun
foggy	rain	thunder
hail	sleet	wind

Holidays

birthday	Halloween	Valentine
Christmas	Hanukkah	Yom Kippur
Easter	Thanksgiving	
Fourth of July	vacation	

Family

aunt	father	mother
brother	grandfather	sister
cousin	grandmother	uncle
daddy	mama	

Insects
bee	grasshopper	worm
bug	spider	
fly	wasp	

Plants, Trees,
etc.
branch	grass	tree
bush	leaf	trunk
corn	nest	wheat
flower	seed	
garden	shrub	

Time
afternoon	morning	today
breakfast	night	tomorrow
dinner	noon	yesterday
evening	now	
lunch	supper	

Body Parts
arm	fingernail	shoulder
bone	foot	skin
cheek	hair	teeth
chest	hand	toe
chin	head	toenail
ear	knee	tongue
elbow	leg	tooth
eye	mouth	tummy
feet	neck	waist
finger	nose	

People
baby	cowboy	girl
boy	doctor	grocer
clown	farmer	Indian
cook	fireman	man

milkman	pilot	waiter
nurse	policeman	waitress
paper boy	teacher	woman

Animals

bear	frog	reindeer
bird	giraffe	robin
butterfly	goat	seal
cat	goose	sheep
chicken	horse	snake
cow	lion	squirrel
dog	monkey	tiger
duck	mouse	turkey
eagle	owl	turtle
elephant	parrot	wolf
fish	pig	zebra
fox	rabbit	

3. *A starter list of pictures showing action*

batting a ball	digging	running
changing a tire	eating	shoveling
cooking	fighting	singing
crying	hammering	sleeping
cutting grass, or	ironing	swinging
barber cutting	jumping	washing
hair	laughing	writing
dancing	painting	

4. *Story pictures* (These you will need when you are well along the way and are working on making good sentences.)
   Pictures of the seasons.
   Pictures of different sports.
   Pictures that tell a story.

5. *Pictures for learning more about big and little.* You can find pictures of many things in two sizes, such as a big

bottle of catsup and a little bottle of catsup, a big boy, a little boy, etc. Put both pictures on one card.

6. Greeting cards often have very good pictures that you can use. Watch for those with a fuzzy surface, such as kittens. Children love to touch these pictures and it helps hold their attention. Look among special cards for children in a card shop. With rubber cement, put *one* picture in the middle of a tag board card. DO NOT put more than one picture on a card. DO NOT use both sides and DO NOT write anything on the cards.

   Tag board is tough and will last a long time. These cards will get a lot of use so you will do well to make them the right way. Keep them clean. Have a large folder or envelope to keep them in. You can even put them in a looseleaf notebook, using a punch to make the holes. DO NOT cover the pictures with plastic. It would help keep the pictures clean, but the shine can be distracting to the child.

C   Making an Easel and Pocket Chart

You will need a rack or easel or pocket chart to hold pictures. This is very necessary for children with Downs Syndrome, for they do not see too well when pictures are shown to them flat on a table.

You can make an easel with two pieces of heavy cardboard, masonite, or plywood. Each piece should be at least 12 inches by 18 inches. Join these boards along the 18-inch side by gluing on a hinge of strips of cloth or strips of leather cut from old gloves. Put a strap or stout cord on each side to keep the easel at a good angle. You can put the easel away easily, as it folds up.

Get one yard of 1-inch elastic. Sew its ends together and slip it over the working side of the easel, about an inch from the bottom. It should be a little bit tight. Slip your pictures under this elastic to keep them from slipping.

Do not decorate. You can paint this easel a soft color or cover with *plain* contact paper but anything else you might add to make it pretty would bother your child. We want him to look at the picture you are working with, nothing else.

D   Using a Tape Recorder and Cassettes

So many of the excellent materials on records are very short and grouped with other bands you do not want to use. Unfortunately as many as seven bands will be on one side of a record, useful for all age levels and interests. You may want to play one band as many as four to eight times in a row to give each child a chance to be a leader. If you try to put the needle back for each repeat, you distract the attention and spoil the flow of the activity.

Set up the record player and the cassette recorder. Simply record the wanted band over and over as many times as you would want to use it. Then use only the cassette for teaching time. This also saves wear and tear on the recording. A battery-operated cassette player is good because you can take it outside for music time.

It is helpful to slow down the record speed when you are recording onto the cassette, if you can avoid getting a droning sound. It's easier for the children as it gives a little more time to respond.

E   Articles and Periodicals That Will Help You

"Communication Boards for Cerebral-palsied Children," by E. T. McDonald and A. S. R. Schultz, in *Journal of Speech and Hearing Disorders* XXXVIII, 1—Reprint can be obtained from Home of the Merciful Savior for Crippled Children
4400 Baltimore Avenue
Philadelphia, Pennsylvania 19104

The Exceptional Parent (practical guidance for parents of children with disabilities). Published 6 times a year.
264 Beacon Street
Boston, Massachusetts 02116

F   Places and People That Will Help You

American Speech and Hearing Association Directory
9030 Old Georgetown Road
Washington, D. C. 20014
National listing of certified speech, language, and hearing clinics and clinicians.

Closer Look
Box 1492
Washington, D. C. 20013
A service set up to help parents of children with developmental disabilities find educational and related services by providing them with information.

Epilepsy Foundation of America
343 South Dearborn Street
Chicago, Illinois 60604

Milton Roy Co.
3500 West De Pauw Boulevard
Suite 1034
Indianapolis, Indiana 46268
"Apple Chart." A technique for visual appraisal of mentally retarded children by L. Lawson M.D. and G. Schoofs M.D.

Medi-check Foundation
2640 Golf Road
Glenview, Illinois 60025
Name tags available for all handicapped persons.

National Association for Downs Syndrome (NADS)
5200 Newport Drive
Rolling Meadows, Illinois 60008

National Association for Retarded Children
2709 Avenue "E" East
Arlington, Texas 76011
Ontario Crippled Children Center
350 Rumsey Road
Toronto, Ontario, Canada M4G 1R8
   More information on communication boards.

G   Toys That Teach (catalogs can be obtained)

American Guidance Service, Inc.
  Publisher's Building
  Circle Pines, Minnesota 55014
Beckley-Cardy Company (includes Milton Bradley materials)
  1900 North Narragansett Avenue
  Chicago, Illinois 60639
Childcraft Education Corporation
  150 East 58th Street
  New York, New York 10022
Community Playthings
  Rifton, New York 12471
Developmental Learning Materials
  7440 Natchez Avenue
  Niles, Illinois 60648
Educational Teaching Aids
  159 West Kinzie Street
  Chicago, Illinois 60610
Follett Instructional Materials
  1010 West Washington Boulevard
  Chicago, Illinois 60607
Ideal School Supply Company
  Oak Lawn, Illinois 60453
Latta's School Supplies and Equipment
  2218 Main Street
  Cedar Falls, Iowa 50613

Mafex Associates, Inc.
  111 Barron Avenue
  Johnstown, Pennsylvania 15706
J. A. Preston Corporation
  71 Fifth Avenue
  New York, New York 10003
Scott, Foresman and Company
  1900 East Lake Avenue
  Glenview, Illinois 60023

H   Books That Will Help You

Baby Learning Through Baby Play by Ira J. Gordon (1970)
  St. Martin's Press
  175 Fifth Avenue
  New York, New York 10010
Child Learning Through Child Play (learning activities for 2-
  and 3-year-olds) (1972)
  St. Martin's Press
  175 Fifth Avenue
  New York, New York 10010
Handling the Young Cerebral-palsied Child at Home by Nancie
  R. Finnie (1968)
  E. P. Dutton & Co., Inc.
  201 Park Avenue South
  New York, New York 10003
Is My Baby All Right? by Virginia Apgar and Joan Beck (1972)
  Trident Press
  630 Fifth Avenue
  New York, New York 10020
Living with Children (new methods for parents and teachers)
  by Gerald R. Patterson and M. Elizabeth Gulion (1968)
  Research Press
  P.O. Box 3177, County Fair Station
  Champaign, Illinois 61820

Talk with Your Hands, Vols. I and II, by David I. Watson
(1973) Available from author and publisher
Route 1
Winneconne, Wisconsin 54986
The Child with Downs Syndrome by David W. Smith and Ann
A. Wilson (1973)
W. B. Saunders Co.
Philadelphia, Pennsylvania 19105
Toilet Training in Less Than a Day by Nathan H. Arzin and
Richard M. Foxx (1974)
Simon & Schuster
630 Fifth Avenue
New York, New York 10020
Toilet Training the Retarded: A Rapid Program for Day- and
Nighttime Independent Toilet Training (1973)
Research Press Co.
P.O. Box 3177, County Fair Station
Champaign, Illinois 61820
Trainable Children by Julia S. Molloy (1972)
The John Day Company
666 Fifth Avenue
New York, New York 10019

Trainable Children includes the Performance Goals Record,
which serves as a record for each individual child's progress.
The Performance Goals Record is also available as a separate
sixty-four page booklet.

I   Books for Fun

Great Big Car & Truck Book		Big Golden Book
Where Is Home?	Clure & Ramsey	Bowmar Early Childhood Series

Me	Clure & Ramsey	Bowmar Early Child-hood Series
Little, Big, Bigger	„ „	„ „
Things I Like to Do	„ „	„ „
How Does It Feel?	„ „	„ „
How Much Is a Penny?	Pop Up Book	Random House
In & Out	„ „	„ „
Counting	„ „	„ „
Going to the Hospital		

Books for the Very Young

See My Toys		Rand McNally Super Book
One, Two, Cock-a-doodle-doo Counting Rhymes and Number Fun		Rand McNally Giant Book
Baby's Things		Platt and Munk Co., Inc.

Beginner Books

Put Me in the Zoo	Robert Lopshire	Beginner Books (Random House)
Cat in the Hat	Dr. Seuss	„ „
Cat in the Hat Comes Back	„	„ „
One Fish, Two Fish	„	„ „
Hop on Pop	„	„ „
Where the Wild Things Are	Maurice Sendak	Harper & Row
There's a Nightmare in My Closet	Mercer Mayer	Dial
Swimmy	Leo Lionni	Pantheon

Try It Again, Sam— Safety When You Walk	Judith Viorst	Lothrop, Lee & Shepard Co.
Noise in the Night	Anne Alexander	Rand McNally
The Museum House Ghosts	Judith Spearing	Atheneum
Maybe a Monster	Martha Alexander	Dial
Little Bear (other Little Bear Books)	E. Minarik	Harper & Row
Do You Know What I'll Do?	Charlotte Zolotow	Harper & Row
Peter's Chair	Ezra Jack Keats	Harper & Row
Wait for William	Marjorie Flack	Houghton Mifflin
Nobody Listens to Andrew	Elizabeth Guilfoile	Follett Pub. Co.
The Little Engine That Could	Watty Piper, George & Doris Hauman	Platt & Munk
Pat the Bunny	Dorothy Kunhardt	Golden Press

Books for Listening

Alexander	Harold Littledale	Parents Magazine Press
I have Feelings	Terry Berger	Behavioral Pub.
One Fine Day	Nonny Hogrogian	Macmillan
Make Way for Ducklings	Robert McCloskey	Viking
May I Bring a Friend?	Beatrice S. De Regniers	Atheneum
Mike Mulligan & His Steam Shovel	Virginia Lee Burton	Houghton Mifflin
The Giving Tree	Shel Silverstein	Harper & Row
Do You Want to Be My Friend?	Eric Carle	T. Y. Crowell

Sometimes I'm Afraid	Jane W. Watson	Western Pub. Co.
Look at Me Now	Jane W. Watson	" "
Sometimes I Get Angry	Jane W. Watson	" "
What Do People Do All Day?	Richard Scarry	Random House
Play on Words	A. & M. Provenson	Random House
I Do Not Like It When My Friend Comes to Visit	Ivan Sherman	Harcourt Brace Jovanovich
The Story of Babar	Jean de Brunhoff	Random House
Fairy Tales and Fables	Pictures by Gyo Fiyekawa Edited by Eve Morel	Grosset & Dunlap
The Story About Ping	Marjorie Flack	Viking
The Snowy Day	Ezra Jack Keats	Viking
Drip, Drop	David Carrick	Macmillan
The First Sign of Winter	Mary Blount Christian	Parents Magazine Press
I Am Happy	Maryann J. Dotts	Abingdon Press
The Daddy Book	Robert Stewart	McGraw-Hill
Push-Pull, Empty-Full	Tara Haban	Macmillan
Head-to-Toe	Anne & Harlow Rockwell	Doubleday
Ira Sleeps Over	Bernard Waber	Houghton Mifflin
How Do I Feel?	Norma Simon	Albert Whitman & Co.
A Very Long Train	Eric Carle	T. Y. Crowell
A Very Long Tail	Eric Carle	T. Y. Crowell

Wait Till the Moon Is Full	Margaret Wise Brown	Harper & Row
Andy: That's My Name	Tomie De Paola	Prentice-Hall
Bedtime for Frances	Russell Hoban	Harper & Row
Angus	Marjorie Flack	Doubleday

J   Records That Will Help You

Bowmar Records
  Singing Fun, Vols. 1 & 2
  More Singing Fun, Vols. 1 & 2
  Songs for Children with Special Needs, Vol. 1
  All About Fall, Winter, Spring, Summer (4 vols.)
Columbia Records
  Put Your Finger in the Air
  Everyone Join in the Game
  Burl Ives Sings
Children's Record Guild
  A Visit to My Little Friend
  Let's Help Mommy
  Eensie Beensie Spider
  When the Sun Shines
  Indoors When It Rains
  Creepy Crawly Caterpillar
  Grandfather's Farm
  Train to the Zoo
  Train to the Farm
Young People's Records
  I'm Dressing Myself
  Men Who Come to Our House
  Trains and Planes
  Out-of-Doors
  Rainy Day

Building a City
When the Sun Shines
Hooray! Today's Your Birthday
Folkways
Call and Response—Ella Jenkins
Counting Songs and Rhythms—Ella Jenkins
You'll Sing a Song and I'll Sing a Song—Ella Jenkins
And One and Two—Ella Jenkins
Rhythm Games and Songs for the Little Ones—Ella Jenkins
John Tracey Clinic
Learning to Listen
Hap Palmer Records
Volumes 1 and 2
Sesame Street Records
(Written by J. Moses, J. Raposo, and J. Stone)

K   Song Books

Learn and Sing, J. Antey, John Day Co.
Treasury of Songs for Little Children, E. Botwin, Hart Pub.
Ella Jenkins Song Book for Children, E. Jenkins, Oak Pub.
Songs to Grow On, B. Landeck, William Sloane Ass.
Fireside Book of Children's Songs, Marie Winn, Simon & Schuster
Hap Palmer Songbook—Vols. 1 & 2
Finger Plays, Golden Press
Let's Do Finger Plays, M. Grayson, Robert B. Luce, Inc.
Wake Up and Sing, Beatrice Landeck and Elizabeth Crook, Edward B. Marks Music Corp.
Music for Exceptional Children, Jack L. Coleman, Irene L. Schoepfle, and Virginia Templeton, Summy-Birchard Co.
Songs for Children, edited by W. J. Glassmacher, Amsco Publishing Co.
Sally Go Round the Sun, Edith Fowke, Doubleday and Co., Inc.

L   Sources for Records, Song Books, and Rhythm Instruments

Lyons Music Co.
530 Riverview Avenue
Elkhart, Indiana 46514

Children's Music Center
5373 West Pico Boulevard
Los Angeles, California 90019

Bowmar
622 Rodier Drive
Glendale, California 91201

Educational Record Sales
157 Chambers Street
New York, N.Y. 10007

Folkways Records
906 Sylvan Avenue
Englewood Cliffs, N. J. 07632

Little Golden Records
1230 Avenue of the Americas
New York, N.Y. 10020

Rhythm Instruments

Rhythm Band, Inc.
P. O. Box 126
Fort Worth, Texas 76101

Be watchful for good "look-at" books and new recordings. Often fascinating books and gadgets turn up in supermarkets, highway plazas, and variety stores.

Glossary of Words You Will Need to Understand

ARTICULATION. The way we put sounds together to say words.

ASSOCIATION. Togetherness—two or more ideas, things, or people doing something together.

ATTENTION. Fastening eyes onto something or someone, listening to some sound, noticing some movement, some taste, smell, or the feel of something.

ATTENTION GETTING. Finding ways to get children to look, listen, touch, taste, smell. (Children try to get attention by their behavior both good and bad. We don't pay attention when it is bad, and we pay attention to good behavior by rewards. In training we use rewards such as food and love to help a child learn to pay attention.)

ATTENTION SPAN. The length of time a child can keep looking, listening, or doing something meaningful.

AUDITORY. About hearing and listening.

AUDITORY TRAINING. Helping a child learn to listen and to understand what he hears.

AWARENESS. Knowing something is going on, or someone or something is near, knowing that something is happening.

BABBLE. Make sounds in a string or chain without saying words. Babble sounds usually start with *b, p,* or *m.*

BEHAVIOR. Anything a living thing does or that is observed which includes movement and thinking.

BLOCK PRINTING. All capital letters: BOYS; EXIT; usually seen in signs.

BODY IMAGE. The mental picture that a person has about his own body, such as where his own foot is and how it attaches to his body, or where his ears are and how they are connected to his body.

BOMBARDING. Attacking with many things to hear, see, touch. If we give a child many things to listen to, he is bombarded with sound. In teaching, we try to bombard him only with sounds that have special meaning to him.

CHAINING. Chaining means putting words together to make phrases and sentences. Chaining also means the way to teach an entire behavior by conditioning, as reinforcing each step separately and then bringing the steps together.

COMMANDS. Words or gestures that tell you to do something in a way that makes you feel you really ought to do it.

COMMUNICATION. Any exchange of ideas.

CONCEPTION. Putting together ideas to get a good answer. Knowing that the meanings of words can be used in different ways. "Chair" means something you sit on. The *conception* of the word "chair" is that you know there are many kinds of chairs but they are all called "chair." Conception of a number means you know how many the number means, and that it is more or less than another number and is made up of more than one combination of numbers: a concept is one idea put together from many meanings.

CONSISTENT. Always the same.

CONSONANT. A letter, or combination of letters, of the alphabet except the vowels *a, e, i, o, u,* and sometimes *y.*

CUE. That which reminds or brings your attention to something.

DELAYED SPEECH. A child should say his first usable words about his first birthday and should put words together about his second birthday. If he does not follow this schedule, it is cause for worry and is called delayed speech.

DEPRIVATION. Not having certain needed things, experiences, or people, because of no money, or no one thinking about this need, or maybe just neglect.

DEVELOPMENT. The way people and things grow.

DISCRIMINATION. Being able to sort stimuli seen, heard, smelled, tasted, and felt. Example: to discriminate between big and little; to discriminate between loud and soft; to discriminate sweet from sour. Or deciding where you want to be, or who or what you want to be with, as it affects only you.

DISTRACTIBLE. Very easily pulled away from what you want attention paid to, often caused by too much noise, too many things around, too many toys in sight.

DISTRACTION. Something that pulls attention away from what you want to do or what you want a child to pay attention to.

DROOL. Allow saliva to run out of the mouth. We usually swallow saliva without even thinking about it. Some children drool, because they don't swallow automatically.

ENVIRONMENT. Everything around you.

EXAMPLE. A pattern to follow or to copy: the pattern or a sample of something a person is expected to do in the same way.

EXPERIENCE. A happening, a doing of an activity that a person is aware of and remembers.

EXPRESSIVE. Putting out an idea, a thought, a feeling.

FRUSTRATION. The feeling of "I just can't do it."

FRUSTRATION LEVEL. Some people get the feeling of not being able to do something more easily than others. One person's point of feeling unable to carry on is that person's frustration level.

GESTURAL LANGUAGE. Exchanging ideas by using gestures or movement instead of spoken words.

GESTURE. A movement usually with hands that sends an idea to another person without using spoken words.

GOALS. The places you score and win. Goals are set in training and education just as goals are marked in athletics. Plans and rules are made to reach the goal agreed upon. Goals are what you hope for and try to get.

HEARING IMPAIRMENT. Not hearing perfectly. Limited ability to hear.

HINT. A little bit of an idea that is given and noticed that helps get an idea across.

IDEA (MEANING). Thoughts, notions, opinions existing in your brain that have special importance to you.

IDEAS. A completely new thought, notion, or opinion which a person thinks up or creates.

IDENTIFYING. Knowing and being sure that some*thing* or some *person* is just that thing or person and nothing else.

IMITATE. Do something just as someone else does it.

INITIAL. The first part, like the first letter of your name; the first sound of a word (the first letter or two); the first step in doing something.

JARGON. Sounds strung together that have some meaning to a child. Sometimes twins talk and understand each other's jargon. Most babies go through a stage of talking in jargon, sort of playing with made-up "words" before they start to use real words.

JOURNAL. A written record, telling about what happened—sort of a diary except that it tells what someone else did.

KINESTHETIC. Movement: when our muscles move any body part, it is kinesthetic action. Kinesthetic means to start movement, to keep it going, and to stop the movement.

LABELING. Attaching a name to something or someone that has definite meaning.

LANGUAGE. A system for putting together meaningful sounds and movements, plus the hearing and understanding of sounds and movements; it is the entire give-and-take of exchanging ideas by meaningful (symbols) sounds, movements, and gestures.

LEARN. To profit from experience and remember so you can use again what the experience taught you; also, to change behavior.

LISTEN. Using your ears to hear by paying attention to the sound you are being expected to hear.

MANUSCRIPT WRITING. Printing words in single unconnected letters: c a t; D i c k; first writing a child learns and the first writing he learns to read.

MEANINGFUL. How much anything affects you; something becomes *meaningful* when you learn that it affects you and is different from other things that affect you.

MORPHEME. A word.

MOTIVATION. A force or desire that makes you want to do something.

MOTOR. Movement or action of the body, not necessarily with thought or planning.

MOTOR CONTROL. Being the boss of how you move your body or your actions.

MOTOR GROWTH. The way you grow in control of the movements of your body.

MOTOR PLANNING. Thinking about how you are going to move any part of your body appropriately.

MOVEMENT. The result of a motor action that puts a body part in another place.

NAME. The sound symbol that belongs to just one thing.

NAMING. Attaching the correct sound symbol to just one thing. This is also called *labeling*.

NEGATIVISTIC. Refusing to go along with any suggestion, command, or idea. It can be a habit to say "no" or to refuse to mind or go along. Some children are negativistic because of so many failures; it is easier to say "no" and not try than to risk another failure.

OBJECTIVES. The targets you are shooting at: the actions, skills, or ideas you set up as the kinds of behavior you want.

OBJECTIVITY. Looking at the target behavior you expect *for its own value*, not as it affects you or how you think it should be.

ORAL. Anything to do with the mouth or with the sound that comes out of the mouth.

ORDER. Putting the first thing first, then the second thing or action, etc. Every thought or act depends upon *order* to have meaning and to be logical. The *order* of communicating is *first* to pay attention, then to listen, then to put the necessary thoughts in the right order, then to act, either by speaking, gesturing, or doing something appropriate.

PALATE. The roof of the mouth: the part between your teeth is called the *hard palate*; the part that slants down over your tongue is the *soft palate*, and this moves quickly to keep the air stream needed for making some sounds from escaping through your nose. If a child is born with the palate open down the middle, it is called a *cleft palate*. Surgery can help correct this. It is very hard to talk clearly with a cleft palate.

PARTS OF SPEECH.

Noun: the *name* of a person, place, or thing.

Pronoun: *a word that takes the place of a noun*, such as *"he"* for John or for Daddy, or *"it"* for cookie.

Verb: a word that tells action or state of being, such as *work, run, am, in.*

Adverb: a word that adds to the meaning of a verb, an adjective, or another adverb: John ran *quickly*—Mary is *very* pretty—or John ran *very quickly.*

Preposition: a word that tells relationship, such as *in* the box, *by* the door, *to* the store, *for* you.

Adjective: a word that describes something.

Conjunction: a connecting word such as *and, or, but.*

Interrogation: *wh* words that ask questions: when, where, which.

Interjection: words put into speech to make it stronger, like *Oh!*; exclamations such as *Aha, Ho Ho Ho.*

PATTERN. A plan or set way of doing something.

PERCEPTIVE. Able to attach meaning to something.

PHONEME. A family of speech sounds written with special symbols /b/, /k/, /θ/, /ð/. The symbol shows the *speech sound* rather than the letter name.

PLAN. A series of ideas put in order so a *goal* can be reached.

POSTURE. The way you line yourself up. Bodily posture is the way you hold your body either standing or sitting.

POTENTIAL. The real ability that can be used.

PREFERENCE. What you would rather use or rather do. You may *prefer* to use your left hand.

PRESCRIPTIVE TEACHING. Teaching planned to help develop areas of learning, such as motor control, memory. Teaching is *prescribed* after learning problems are found (like a doctor writes a prescription after he examines you to find out what is wrong).

PROBE. To find a way to help complete an action or idea. We *probe* a child to complete a word or idea by helping him find a start or completing an unfinished word or sentence.

PROCEDURE. The spelled-out, step-by-step way to do something.

QUALIFY. To add meaning to a word by using another word that makes it more special: such as *big* ball, *square* table, *yellow* sweater, *hard* candy, *wet* pants. Usually adjectives.

RANDOM. Any which way: wild motions or wild guessing without planning or much idea behind the action.

RECEPTION. Receiving, taking in through your senses: hearing, seeing, touching, smelling, tasting.

RECEPTIVE. Able to receive through your senses: hearing, seeing, touching, smelling, tasting.

REPETITION: Doing something over again and again.

REWARD. That which is satisfying to you for which you are willing to expend effort.

RHYTHM. Repeated beat like your heartbeats. The time between the beats or accents can be short or long or varied according to a pattern or plan.

ROUTINE. A planned sequence of events, or experiences that

are set and do not change very often. You do the series as you are expected to do it.

SATISFY. Reach an end result that fits the task or that makes you or someone else feel good about it.

SATURATION. Soaked full of something, like a sponge full of water. People can get soaked full of too much being put upon them. A child can take just so much in one lesson; you may not think he is really saturated; but if he can't do any more at that time, he has reached a point of saturation for that time.

SCALE. A way to measure how much, how many, how far. A *language development scale* lists steps along the way to use language; then you can measure how far along a child is.

SENSORY. Pertaining to the senses: hearing, seeing, touching, smelling, tasting.

SEQUENCE. One thing after another: usually in order of what should be done before the next thing is to be done.

SHAPING. Molding simple behavior into more complicated behaviors.

SIGNING. The use of the hands in gesture or finger spelling to convey an idea.

SOCIAL. The things you do that let you get along with people. To be social you cannot be disagreeable, selfish, mean, dirty. *Social growth* is learning to do the things that make people want to be with you.

SOUND SYMBOL. One little piece of sound that means something. A *symbol* is something that stands for something else. You hear or see the word "dog." *Dog* is a *sound symbol* for the special animal we have learned is labeled dog. Spoken words are all *sound symbols*.

SPEECH. Production of sounds put together in such a way that a certain meaning is intended to be understood by another person.

SPONTANEOUS. Happening without help from outside: ideas or action starting from inside yourself.

STIMULATE. To make some things happen. You push a button (stimulate) and a doorbell rings. You stimulate a child to do something by planning ways to get him to do what you want him to do.

STIMULATION. What made you do something.

STIMULUS. That which reminds us or steers us to behave in a certain way.

SYMBOL. Something that stands for something else: an arrow is a symbol that stands for the words "go this way." A plus mark ($+$) is a symbol that means "add." Written numbers or spoken names are symbols for that special amount of things. The letters of the alphabet are symbols that are put together to make words. Words are symbols for things, ideas, actions.

TACTILE. Touch. You get a message, a *tactile* message, when you touch something. The thing is soft, hard, cold, scratchy, heavy, sticky, wet.

TBA. TOTAL BODY ACTIVITY. A planned program to teach a child to manage and control his body and to serve as a base for learning that parts of our bodies have names, that *where* we move and *how* we move have special words that we can use in daily living. TBA is a base for learning to communicate. The child's own body is used to start his understanding of sound symbols, or words.

TECHNIQUE. A special way of doing something that is carefully studied before being used, so it will do the job it is intended to do.

TONGUE THRUST. Forward movement of the tongue while swallowing. Found in all very young children; but as the child grows, he loses this movement. (Often related to abnormal bite and articulation problems.)

TOTAL COMMUNICATION. Gestural language or signs with the spoken word or words.

VERBALIZATION. Putting ideas into words.

VISUAL. Seeing.

VISUAL SYMBOL. A symbol whose meaning is seen rather than heard or touched: a smile, frown, gesture, signs, written words, letters, numbers.

VOCABULARY. A collection of words: the total of all the

words a person uses, or a special vocabulary is a collection of all the words used on one special subject.

VOCAL. Sounds uttered, spoken, sung, so they can be heard.

VOICE. Sound uttered by living things, especially by people in speech, song, crying, shouting, hollering.

VOLUME. How much anything holds or how much is the amount of loudness or softness you use.

VOWEL. In English-American speech *a, e, i, o, u,* and sometimes *y*. These letters are controlled by the position and tenseness of your tongue and the vibrations from your voice box. Your lips and jaw do not work to make vowel sounds.

WORD MEANINGS. The exact idea you get from the words you hear or see written.

Index